BEST EASY BIRD GUIDE
Cape Cod

HELP US KEEP THIS GUIDE UP TO DATE

Every effort has been made by the author and editors to make this guide as accurate and useful as possible. However, many things can change after a guide is published.

We would appreciate hearing from you concerning your experiences with this guide and how you feel it could be improved and kept up to date. While we may not be able to respond to all comments and suggestions, we'll take them to heart, and we'll also make certain to share them with the author. Please send your comments and suggestions to the following address:

FalconGuides
Reader Response/Editorial Department
246 Goose Lane
Guilford, CT 06437

Thanks for your input!

Best Easy Bird Guide Series

BEST EASY BIRD GUIDE
Cape Cod

A Field Guide to the Birds of Cape Cod

RANDI MINETOR
Photography by NIC MINETOR

GUILFORD, CONNECTICUT

An imprint of The Rowman & Littlefield Publishing Group, Inc.
4501 Forbes Blvd., Ste. 200
Lanham, MD 20706
www.rowman.com
Falcon and FalconGuides are registered trademarks and Make Adventure Your Story is a trademark of The Rowman & Littlefield Publishing Group, Inc.

Distributed by NATIONAL BOOK NETWORK

Copyright © 2021 The Rowman & Littlefield Publishing Group, Inc.

Maps by The Rowman & Littlefield Publishing Group, Inc.
All interior photographs by Nic Minetor
Parts of a bird drawing on p. xxii by Todd Telander

British Library Cataloguing-in-Publication Information available

Library of Congress Cataloging in Publication Data
Names: Minetor, Randi, author. | Minetor, Nic, photographer.
Title: Best easy bird guide Cape Cod : a field guide to the birds of Cape Cod / Randi Minetor ; photography by Nic Minetor.
Description: Lanham : FalconGuides, 2021. | Series: Best Easy Bird Guide series | "Distributed by NATIONAL BOOK NETWORK"—T.p. verso. | Includes bibliographical references and index. | Summary: "Best Easy Bird Guide Cape Cod opens the world of birding to the novice and expert in this complete guide to getting the most out of birding in Cape Cod"—Provided by publisher.
Identifiers: LCCN 2020038902 (print) | LCCN 2020038903 (ebook) | ISBN 9781493055203 (Trade Paperback) | ISBN 9781493055210 (ePub)
Subjects: LCSH: Bird watching—Massachusetts—Cape Cod—Guidebooks. | Cape Cod Bay (Mass.)—Guidebooks.
Classification: LCC QL684.M4 M56 2021 (print) | LCC QL684.M4 (ebook) | DDC 598.072/3474492—dc23
LC record available at https://lccn.loc.gov/2020038902
LC ebook record available at https://lccn.loc.gov/2020038903

♾™ The paper used in this publication meets the minimum requirements of American National Standard for Information Sciences—Permanence of Paper for Printed Library Materials, ANSI/NISO Z39.48-1992.

CONTENTS

CONTENTS

ACKNOWLEDGMENTS

Birders are some of the best people in the world, eager to share information about sightings, to enhance one another's experience and understanding of birds in the wild, and to "get everyone on the bird," whether they're leading a field trip or just happen to be standing there looking at an interesting bird when others arrive. When we contacted birders in New England and closer to our upstate New York home to help us find the birds to photograph for this series, they shared their knowledge willingly, gave us some terrific tips for finding particularly elusive birds, recommended places for lunch, led us to known breeding sites, and even brought us into their own backyards. There are too many of these folks to list—and some of them never told us their names—but we are grateful to just about every birder we have ever met.

As always, the team at FalconGuides has produced a great book: senior acquisitions editor David Legere, production editor Ellen Urban, copy editor Paulette Baker, graphic artist Melissa Evarts, cartographer Melissa Baker, and proofreader Ashley Benning. Our brilliant agent Regina Ryan continues to keep our publishing careers on track, taking extraordinary care of us so we can pursue our passions throughout the region and beyond.

Finally, to the friends and family who support us in all our efforts, we cannot say enough about your generosity of spirit when it comes to our literary endeavors. Ken Horowitz, Rose-Anne Moore, Martin Winer, Bruce Barton, Lisa Jaccoma, the late Bil Walters, Christine Tattersall, Martha and Peter Schermerhorn, Ruth Watson, John King, Cindy Blair, Paula and Rich Landis, neighbor Pam Bartemus, and all the others scattered across the country: You make every chapter fun, and there are no words strong enough to express our gratitude.

INTRODUCTION

It's just a narrow peninsula, about 65 miles long and barely 20 miles wide at its thickest point, but Cape Cod's 400-plus miles of coastline along Cape Cod Bay and the Atlantic Ocean make it one of the hottest birding spots in the entire New England region. New birders who find their way here often discover seabirds and shorebirds for the first time, rapidly ticking off a dozen duck species, six or more warbler species of the beach scrublands, a variety of sparrows, sandpipers and plovers running back and forth along the beaches, and varieties of gulls and terns that never find their way farther inland. For first-timers, Cape Cod is a birding wonderland; for those who return again and again in different seasons, the peninsula provides plenty of opportunities to explore somewhere new and see migrating and overwintering birds.

This book provides photos and descriptions of the one hundred most common birds on Cape Cod, as well as suggested hot spots where you will be most likely to find them in the right season. Cape Cod has attracted more than 300 bird species to its shores, forests, lakes, ponds, and open habitats; this book will help you identify the ones found most frequently.

Geography and Habitats

Cape Cod contains a landmass of 1,306 square miles, combining more than 400 miles of sandy coastline and an ecosystem known as the Massachusetts Coastal Pine Barrens. Pine barrens contain dry, acidic soil in which only a handful of plant species can thrive—mostly spindly grasses and low shrubs, as well as small to midsize pine trees and some other conifers. Just 306 feet in elevation at its highest point, the Cape invites Atlantic winds to blow across it strongly at any time of year, its arid length acting as a protective barrier for the mainland in the face of violent storms in late summer and fall. Overall, however, its climate is surprisingly mild, tempered by ocean breezes that keep summer temperatures in the 70s and 80s Fahrenheit and winter in the 20s and 30s.

Newcomers to the Cape may not understand the terminology used by locals to describe various locations along its length.

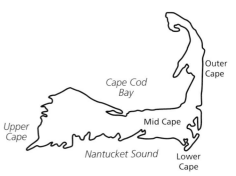

- Despite its location at the southwest end of the peninsula, the area just across Cape Cod Canal from the mainland is known as the Upper Cape. The towns of Bourne, Falmouth, Sandwich, and Mashpee are in this section.
- The Mid-Cape is the midsection of the peninsula's southern length, including Barnstable, Yarmouth, and Dennis.
- The "elbow" of the peninsula is called the Lower Cape, with Brewster, Harwich, and Chatham in this section.
- From Orleans and Eastham up to Provincetown, the section stretching northward is called the Outer Cape.

The Coasts

The beaches of Cape Cod offer an unusually rich birding experience. Cape Cod National Seashore, stretching along the Outer Cape from Eastham to the tip of Race Point, protects more than 60 miles of untrammeled, open beach, the most popular of which are Nauset Light and Coast Guard Beaches near Eastham, at the park's southern end. Here you can find gulls, terns, sanderlings and other small shorebirds and protected areas for breeding piping plovers, the most endangered bird species in the park. Watch for areas enclosed by ropes, with signs that explain the breeding habits of these sand-colored birds and the need to help sustain their numbers.

Race Point, at the seashore's northern end beyond Provincetown, can provide an extraordinary pelagic birding experience. Pelagic birds breed and feed out at sea and rarely if ever approach the mainland, usually building or digging their nests on islands many miles offshore. In some years, schools of tiny fish called menhaden swim very close to Race Point and its beach, however, and the shearwaters and alcids follow them right up to the beach, providing spectacular viewing for lucky birders who manage to be there when it happens. The fall of 2017 brought this phenomenon so close to the beach that shearwaters, jaegers, and dovekies came within a few feet of onlookers.

The western edge of Cape Cod offers beaches, inlets, and harbors along Cape Cod Bay, where long-legged waders and other birds that prefer warmer water may stop for the summer. Wellfleet Bay Wildlife Sanctuary preserves salt marshes and coastal woodlands that regularly host great and snowy egrets, great blue heron, green heron, piping plover, willet, and all the more common shorebirds from midsummer to fall. Here laughing gulls are the dominant black-headed species, and least and common terns, prairie warbler, swamp sparrow, and a wide variety of songbirds make their summer home.

The Woodlands

Cape Cod National Seashore protects some isolated stands of forest, including the Beech Forest at Race Point and the Atlantic White Cedar Swamp near the Marconi Station site. Both of these have easily walkable trails, but insect repellent is more than a must—it's a dire necessity. Mosquitoes are thick and thirsty in these woodlands, and while this is critically important to attracting insect-eating songbirds, it can also make for a decidedly unpleasant hiking experience. Be sure to apply a good coat of repellent and to wear a long-sleeved shirt and long pants if you are visiting in spring or summer.

Farther south in the Upper and Mid-Cape, Bell's Neck Conservation Lands in Harwich and Nickerson State Park in Brewster both offer the opportunity to bird in second-growth woodlands. While wooded areas are the exception rather than the norm, local land trusts have managed to preserve Coy's Brook Woodlands in Harwich, Tobey Woodlands in Dennis, and Shallow Pond Woodlands in Falmouth, among others.

Virtually every forest or thick woods contains all four resident woodpeckers—downy, hairy, red-bellied, and northern flicker—as well as spring and summer residents including yellow and yellow-rumped warbler; white-throated, chipping, and song sparrows; blue jay; northern cardinal; Baltimore oriole; Carolina and house wrens; and colorful songbirds. Wood thrushes fill the woods with their flutelike songs. Wild turkeys have been restored to habitat where they were considered extirpated a century ago. It's rare to hike through a woodland area without encountering at least one of these massive birds or hearing their cheery, burbling gobble somewhere in the understory.

Spring is an exciting time in the Cape Cod woodlands, with more than thirty species of warblers arriving in late April and throughout May, many of them passing through on their way to breeding grounds farther north. Fox and Lincoln's sparrows, rusty blackbird, and Swainson's and gray-cheeked thrushes are among the less common migrants that rest and refuel before proceeding northward along the Atlantic flyway. If you'd like to know more about all the migrating birds that pass through this region, our comprehensive book *Birding New England* provides photos and life histories about every bird that stops in this area regularly.

Open Country

Salt marshes and scrubland adjacent to beaches host many kinds of wildlife, providing food and habitat for breeding birds and shelter for birds that overwinter here. Sparrows, red-winged blackbird, eastern kingbird, eastern bluebird, prairie warbler, eastern towhee, and common yellowthroat are all dependent on open lands from spring through fall. In spring, the marshes attract flocks of shorebirds and dabbling ducks, as well as great and snowy egrets, great blue heron, green heron, and thousands of Canada geese. Rarer birds like whimbrel, godwits, glossy ibis, and a range of others also find their way to these areas on their way north in spring or south in early fall, making every trip to a marsh a birding adventure.

Cape Cod offers birders a wealth of experiences and the opportunity to locate many varieties. A visit here any time of year will produce a wide range of sightings—and for residents, every season brings a new scavenger hunt, a chance to see birds that have become as familiar as old friends and to track down one of the tricky species that eludes even the most avid and experienced birder.

Optics and How to Choose Them

If you are new to birding and have not yet acquired your own binoculars or decided on the need for a spotting scope, we offer some basic guidance:

1. **Yes, you need binoculars.** Birds rarely land close enough to give you a good, satisfying look, especially if you're examining an unfamiliar wing pattern, an alternate seasonal plumage, or details you've never seen in person before. Binoculars are key to your enjoyment of the birds, but which binoculars are right for you? Here are the most important things to understand when purchasing a pair for your birding enjoyment:

   - **Look for the magnification and diameter formula,** usually stamped on the focus knob. For example, it may say 7 x 35, 8 x 42, or 10 x 40. The first number indicates the number of times the binoculars magnify the image of the bird—so if the first number is "8," it means you will see the bird at eight times its normal size. You may believe, then, that a magnification of 10 or more would be the best for your purposes, but before you leap to buy such a pair, try it out in person. You may find that 10x binoculars are too heavy to hold still, making the additional magnification an expensive waste. Many birders are most comfortable with a factor of 8.
   - **The diameter number** (35, 40, 42, or 50) tells you how much light comes through the large end of the binoculars. The number is the diameter of the lens itself, and the larger it is, the brighter and clearer the image will be when it reaches your eye. Binoculars with a larger diameter are especially good in low-light situations, like when

you're trying to see the mating dance of the American woodcock at dusk or you're attempting to spot a barred owl calling in a dim forest.

- **The secret is the multicoating.** Why are your grandfather's 10 x 50 binoculars, purchased in the 1960s, not nearly as good for birding as a modern pair at 7 x 35? Optics technology has come a long way over the past fifty years, eliminating distortions like the blue-and-yellow fringe around objects you may see through your granddad's pair. "Fully multicoated" means every piece of glass inside and out—as many as eighteen surfaces—is layered with coatings that reduce glare, distortion, fringing, and other issues that can keep you from seeing a bird clearly.

- **Get past the sticker shock.** Cheap binoculars are not going to cut it in the field, so if you're a committed birder and want the best experience possible, you're going to have to spend a little money. There's good news on this front, however: Several top manufacturers have developed excellent binoculars at a price point of about $250, so you don't need to stretch for a top-of-the-line pair in the $1,200 range to have perfectly serviceable optics.

2. **Do you need a spotting scope?** It's a valid question, especially if you're new to birding, and one you need to answer in your own time. To get an idea of the possibilities a scope opens up for you, participate in a field trip with your local birding association and look through several of the scopes other birders use. Remember how you felt the first time you saw a bird through a good pair of binoculars? The leap from binoculars to a scope is equally dramatic. If you do decide to purchase your own scope, keep in mind that the tripod is every bit as important as the magnification and diameter—on a windy day or when you're standing on a busy boardwalk, you'll be glad you chose a slightly heavier, more stable tripod that keeps your scope from vibrating.

Bird Classifications

The American Ornithological Society and the American Birding Association have teams of experts who have spent years determining the exact biological category each bird belongs in, what family of birds it belongs to within that category, and what its taxonomic (Latin) name should be. This is critically important work for our scientific understanding of birds, their evolution, and the discovery of new species through DNA analysis and other methods.

Bird taxonomy informed this book, but we also relied on our own field experience, gathered through more than thirty-five years of birding, and our use of a wide range of field guides. In this book we have endeavored to group birds within their taxonomic families, but also in a manner that will make it easy to compare one bird to another for purposes of identification. So you'll find all the swimming birds grouped together, as well as all the wading birds, the raptors, and so on. This enhances the usability of this guide, allowing you to focus on studying the bird's field marks in relation to others in the same general habitat.

Seasonal Plumage and Other Mysteries

As if the process of identifying each bird were not confounding enough, most birds lose their bright breeding plumage once the mating season is over. All birds molt at least once a year, dropping their old feathers and replacing them with new ones, but not all of them change the look of their plumage from one season to the next. When they do, it can result in considerable confusion for birders struggling to identify individuals in a mixed flock of what the 1980 Peterson *Field Guide to the Birds* famously dubbed "confusing fall warblers."

To help you sort out the field marks (or lack of them) when the birds make it the hardest to do so, we have provided detailed descriptions of nonbreeding plumage for each of the birds that make this transition. Many fall warblers look nearly identical in their nonbreeding plumage, with perhaps a single feature that differs, so you can make careful comparisons of the descriptions to determine which species you may be seeing. Remember that the bird's habitat, food choices, song, and behavior are still the guiding factors to its identification, especially when the plumage provides few clues.

Many waterfowl go through two periods of molt each year, based on their nesting and breeding schedule. Male ducks lose their bright feathers soon after nesting, changing over to a drab appearance called "eclipse" plumage as early as the last week of June. This is particularly evident in wood ducks, which go from a coat of many colors to a brown mantle with a white patch at the throat. In early winter, when other species of birds are still cloaked for fall, male wood ducks and other waterfowl regain their stunning plumage in preparation for attracting a mate.

Some birds—particularly those that spend winter on the northern Atlantic Ocean after breeding near or above the Arctic Circle—rarely if ever appear in their breeding plumage on Cape Cod. For these, we have provided photos of the birds as you will see them during their winter sojourn, rather than raising the expectation that you may view them in their brighter breeding mantle.

Birding by Ear

One of the most important skills you need to bird in any area of the world is an ability to identify birds by song. It's not as difficult as you may think—the more you listen in the field and practice with recordings, the clearer it will become that each bird has a distinctly different way of expressing itself.

We have provided phonetic transcriptions of each bird's song or call in this book, with popular phrases and mnemonics to help you learn some of the most common and familiar calls. That being said, there is no substitute for a good smartphone app that puts every bird's song in your pocket. Some apps serve as an adjunct to field guides (or are part of a field guide app, such as iBird Pro, National Geographic Birds, Sibley eGuide, Audubon Birds Pro, and Peterson Birds), so you can choose a bird and listen to all the variations of its song. Others actually teach you how to tell one bird's song from another and how to remember each song. Highly recommended teaching apps include Larkwire, Chirp!, and IKnowBirdSongs; each is available for a onetime fee. Many of these apps use songs from the Macaulay Library at the Cornell Laboratory of Ornithology, one of the most respected and extensive resources for bird information in North America.

If you are daunted by the idea of learning birdsongs, let us say this: You will be amazed at how much time it saves you in the field. Start by learning the ten most common birds in your own backyard—for example, house sparrow, northern cardinal, blue jay, American goldfinch, American robin, red-winged blackbird, mourning dove, white-breasted nuthatch, house wren, and house finch. Each of these birds has a distinctive song, making this sampler an excellent starting point in learning what makes one song different from another. With these ten (or ten others you choose) firmly in your mind, you'll be able to identify these birds in the field whether you actually see them or not, allowing you to apply more of your time and effort to finding more unusual birds on each field trip.

Rare, Endangered, and Extirpated Species

Setting expectations in advance will help you come home from any birding excursion with the satisfaction that you saw what you came to see. That's why we need to be up front about the birds that are very difficult to see on Cape Cod, as well as the birds that were once, but are no longer, part of the landscape.

Four species that once lived in New England are now extinct: passenger pigeon (the last known individual in the world died in 1914), Labrador duck (1878), great auk (1852), and Eskimo curlew (1987). Others that were once reported here fairly regularly are rarely seen in New England at all, so a single sighting can become a regional bird event—for example, gray partridge, hoary redpoll, or loggerhead shrike.

In addition, Massachusetts has its own current list of species that are endangered or of special concern. Sightings of these are possible, but they may be difficult to locate even in their accustomed hot spots: American bittern, Arctic tern, barn owl, common gallinule, golden-winged warbler, Henslow's sparrow, long-eared owl, roseate tern, sedge wren, short-eared owl, upland sandpiper, and vesper sparrow. As this book provides photos and descriptions of the one hundred most common birds on Cape Cod, you won't find photos of these rarer species here.

Why are these birds—some of which are fairly common in other parts of the country—becoming scarce in Massachusetts? The effects of the changing climate already have had an impact in this region, and forecasts by scientists including those at Mass Audubon paint an alarming picture. With warmer air temperatures throughout the year, shorter cold seasons, more rain, more severe storms, and rising sea levels, climate change "is changing the fundamental way ecosystems work," a 2017 Mass Audubon report says. Warmer winters, the report continues, "cause shifts in the way that marine food webs work, which will cascade through the environment and affect fish populations and, in turn, fish-eating birds."

The rising temperatures can affect when trees produce leaves in spring and when insects emerge, which can mean that bird migration may no longer coincide with peaks in food availability. In addition, the cost of rising sea levels is obvious: Loss of salt marsh habitat along the coastline can leave shorebirds, waterfowl, and long-legged waders with nowhere to nest and feed, while increased storm activity can flood marshes, washing away nests and drowning tiny organisms that live in shallow water and serve as food to wading birds. It's a frightening picture, but the truth is that bird populations are under siege.

You will see the effects of climate change as you bird your way through Cape Cod. In fact, if you've been delaying a trip to some of the areas along the edges of the Cape, especially Monomoy National Wildlife Refuge and other island habitats, it's time to treat yourself to a visit. Rising sea levels may make these areas inhospitable to the bird populations they now support—and some refuges may be in danger of disappearing altogether.

Birding Ethics in the Age of Social Media

While your life list is your own and you have the option of counting whatever bird sightings you choose, some aspects of ethical birding are not optional. The American Birding Association provides this Code of Birding Ethics, and you will find that the vast majority of birders you meet follow this to the letter.

American Birding Association Code of Birding Ethics

Reproduced with permission. For more information about the American Birding Association, visit aba.org.

1. **Promote the welfare of birds and their environment.**
   1(a) Support the protection of important bird habitat.

   1(b) Avoid stressing birds or exposing them to danger; exercise restraint and caution during observation, photography, sound recording, or filming.

   - Limit the use of recordings and other methods of attracting birds, and never use such methods in heavily birded areas or for attracting any species that is Threatened, Endangered, of Special Concern, or is rare in your local area.

   - Keep well back from nests and nesting colonies, roosts, display areas, and important feeding sites. In such sensitive areas, if there is a need for extended observation, photography, filming, or recording, try to use a blind or hide, and take advantage of natural cover.

   - Use artificial light sparingly for filming or photography, especially for close-ups.

   1(c) Before advertising the presence of a rare bird, evaluate the potential for disturbance to the bird, its surroundings, and other people in the area, and proceed only if access can be controlled, disturbance minimized, and permission has been obtained from private landowners. The sites of rare nesting birds should be divulged only to the proper conservation authorities.

   1(d) Stay on roads, trails, and paths where they exist; otherwise, keep habitat disturbance to a minimum.

2. **Respect the law, and the rights of others.**
   2(a) Do not enter private property without the owner's explicit permission.

   2(b) Follow all laws, rules, and regulations governing use of roads and public areas, both at home and abroad.

2(c) Practice common courtesy in contacts with other people. Your exemplary behavior will generate goodwill with birders and non-birders alike.

3. **Ensure that feeders, nest structures, and other artificial bird environments are safe.**

3(a) Keep dispensers, water, and food clean and free of decay or disease. It is important to feed birds continually during harsh weather.

3(b) Maintain and clean nest structures regularly.

3(c) If you are attracting birds to an area, ensure the birds are not exposed to predation from cats and other domestic animals or dangers posed by artificial hazards.

4. **Group birding, whether organized or impromptu, requires special care.**

Each individual in the group, in addition to the obligations spelled out in Items 1 and 2, has responsibilities as a Group Member:

4(a) Respect the interests, rights, and skills of fellow birders, as well as people participating in other legitimate outdoor activities. Freely share your knowledge and experience, except where code 1(c) applies. Be especially helpful to beginning birders.

4(b) If you witness unethical birding behavior, assess the situation and intervene if you think it prudent. When interceding, inform the person(s) of the inappropriate action and attempt, within reason, to have it stopped. If the behavior continues, document it and notify appropriate individuals or organizations.

Group Leader Responsibilities [amateur and professional trips and tours]:

4(c) Be an exemplary ethical role model for the group. Teach through word and example.

4(d) Keep groups to a size that limits impact on the environment and does not interfere with others using the same area.

4(e) Ensure everyone in the group knows of and practices this code.

4(f) Learn and inform the group of any special circumstances applicable to the areas being visited (e.g., no audio playback allowed).

4(g) Acknowledge that professional tour companies bear a special responsibility to place the welfare of birds and the benefits of public knowledge ahead of the company's commercial interests. Ideally, leaders should keep track of tour sightings, document unusual occurrences, and submit records to appropriate organizations.

Why follow this code? Naturally, it's good for the birds, even if it means you don't have the opportunity to get a good look at a rarity or add a bird to your life list. There's another facet we must take into consideration in the age of social media, however: Infractions can be photographed or recorded, and your peccadillo in the field can become a matter of indelible public record.

For example, during the snowy owl irruption of 2018, a birder in upstate New York observed a younger, less-experienced birder attempting to get a photo of an owl perched on a shrub in a snow-covered field. While birders following the ABA Code of Ethics knew they should stay at the roadside and view the owl through a scope from a considerable distance, this fairly new birder decided to cross the field and get much closer to the bird. Not only was this unhealthy for the bird, which may have flown a long distance overnight in search of lemmings that were not available farther north, but this birder also trespassed on private land.

The mature birder, observing this, whipped out her smartphone and made a video of the young birder crossing the field. She posted this on the local birders' Facebook page. Page members could not see the young birder's face, but some recognized his clothing and gear and identified him by name. In minutes—before the birder left the field—he had been "outed" as unethical. Comments ran rampant, some arguing that the young man was new to birding and didn't know that he'd proceeded in an unethical manner; others chastising the birder who took the video for not stopping him from crossing the field. Still others suggested that the young man be reported to the local department of environmental conservation or the regional US Fish and Wildlife Service office.

The final outcome of this incident was not published on Facebook, but chances are this young man received many a scolding at subsequent field trips and suspicious looks whenever he ran into a birder who recognized him. The moral is simple: Behave yourself in the field, and put the welfare of the bird before your zeal to check off a sighting or get a great photo. It's the right thing to do for the birds, and it will keep you from getting a bad reputation that lives forever on the internet.

HOW TO USE THIS GUIDE

On each page, you'll find photographs and details that will help you identify the birds you see and determine the best places to find them.

Field marks: In addition to the photos, we have listed the features that differentiate this bird from others. These descriptions begin with a breeding male and are followed by breeding female and any changes for nonbreeding plumage.

Size: The bird's approximate length (L) or height (H) (for tall wading birds like great blue heron) and wingspan (WS) can be important to its identification.

Similar species: As every birder knows, misidentifications are easy to make. We've simplified the process of elimination by providing the key field marks that may indicate that the bird in your sights is not what you think it is.

Season: The time of year you are most likely to see this bird.

Habitat: Birds wander, but they tend to stay close to their nesting sites and to the areas in which they can find food. We provide the most likely habitat for each.

Food source: This will help you determine whether the bird you seek can find its food in the place you're looking. If you don't see evergreen trees with cones, for example, you're not likely to find crossbills.

Nest: Many of the birds in this book do not nest and breed on Cape Cod. For the ones that do, we've provided the probable nest location—in a tree above 50 feet, for example, or on the ground among reeds and tall grasses.

Call: Nothing beats a recording of an actual birdcall, but the phonetic transcriptions you find here may help you match the kind of call you're hearing so that you can narrow down the possibilities for identification. If male and female have different calls, both are provided.

Hot spots: Here you'll find three to five places on Cape Cod where the bird has been seen season after season or year after year. To determine these hot spots, we toured Cape Cod and visited dozens of birding locations, using our personal experience to determine which places yielded the most sightings and provided a high-quality experience in general. We rejected some sites because they were on private or restricted property, they did not provide a safe place to leave a vehicle, or there was no clear path to the birding location.

I also applied science to the task. I used the sightings reported by tens of thousands of birders in eBird, the crowdsourced database developed and managed by the Cornell Laboratory of Ornithology at Cornell University. Rather than delving back through decades of sightings to find where a bird may have been seen historically, I used data collected over the past three years—providing you with the most up-to-date information about where each bird has been seen most recently and consistently. I looked not only for a long list of sightings of a specific species—these, after all, could all be a single bird seen by a large group on one day—but also for year-after-year sightings of that species, a sign that this hot spot drew the desired species consistently.

You will see that many of the hot spots are cited repeatedly: for example, Race Point Beach, Wellfleet Bay Wildlife Sanctuary, Monomoy National Wildlife Refuge, Fort Hill, Bell's Neck Conservation Area, Long Pasture Wildlife Sanctuary, Frances A. Crane Wildlife Management Area, Mashpee Pond, Pogorelc Sanctuary, and many others. We hope this emphasis speaks to the obvious point: These are the best places to bird to find the greatest number of species in one place. Make note of these as you plan your exploration of Cape Cod.

Each of these hot spots includes the nearest town or city, and GPS coordinates for the entrance or location. (Please note: GPS coordinates *do not* mean, "Stand here and you'll see this bird." They are simply provided to make certain you reach the right wildlife refuge, forest, beach, lake, or parking area.)

Range map: This map shows the season and areas of Cape Cod in which the bird is usually seen.

Map Key

Winter

Migration (spring or fall)

Summer (breeding)

Year-round

Birders know well that no sighting is guaranteed. Birds have minds of their own, and they can decide to move hours or seconds before you arrive; they also may choose a new place to rest, feed, and raise their young from one year to the next. We have provided information about the type of habitat each bird prefers so that you can search in suitable places if the birds reject a particular beach, a salt marsh disappears as the sea level rises, or a section of forest does not produce a hardy cone crop in a given year.

PARTS OF A BIRD

We have used plain English terms throughout the descriptions in this book, but this illustration will help you determine which area we mean.

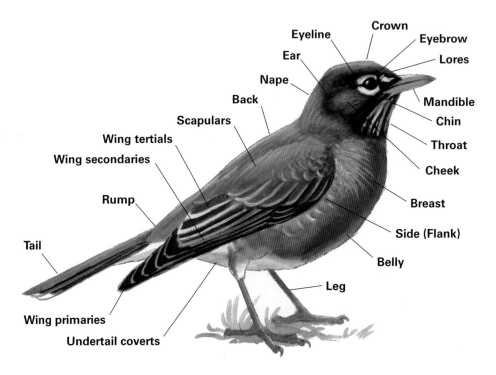

LOON

COMMON LOON
Gavia immer

A spring and fall migrant in harbors and on secluded ponds and lakes, this loon seeks the Atlantic coast's open water in winter.

Field marks: Black head, black bill, red eye, pinstriped collar ending in a black band, striking checkerboard pattern on back, white breast. Nonbreeding plumage is slate gray with a white eye ring and collar-like white notch around neck.

Size: L: 26"–32", WS: 41"–52"

Similar species: Red-throated loon is smaller and grayer, with thin bill and more white on face. Double-crested cormorant is all black with a yellow bill.

Season: Winter on Outer Cape; year-round on Upper Cape

Habitat: Harbors, bays, freshwater ponds and lakes in migration; coastal waters, lakes and other open water in winter

Food source: Fish

Nest: In secluded spots along lakeshores with easy access to water

Call: Plaintive trill that has become synonymous with wilderness: a tremolo of ten or twelve beats in quick succession; also a yodeling call: *woooWAHwha, woooWAHwah*

Hot spots: Race Point Beach, Provincetown, 42.0691855 / -70.2381706; Nauset Light Beach, Eastham, 41.8586304 / -69.9517322; Monomoy National Wildlife Refuge, Chatham, 41.6568485 / -69.9582152; Long Pasture Wildlife Sanctuary, Barnstable, 41.70703 / -70.27171; Sandwich Marina, Sandwich, 41.7736623 / -70.4996526

1

GREBES

RED-NECKED GREBE
Podiceps grisegena
Striking in all plumages, this grebe prefers wide-open waters throughout the region.

Field marks: Heavy, long yellow bill and black cap year-round. Breeding adult has deep reddish throat and white face and jaw. Winter plumage is muted gray with brownish neck.

Size: L: 18"–20", WS: 24"

Similar species: Horned grebe has yellow tufts on each side of its head.

Season: Winter

Habitat: Large lakes, open ocean

Food source: Fish, aquatic insects, some shellfish, amphibians

Nest: On the water in a floating mound of gathered plant material (This grebe does not nest in New England.)

Call: Generally silent in winter. Call is a series of staccato sounds beginning with squeals and continuing to *ih-ih-ih-ih-ih-ih* notes, finally winding down to a low chuckle.

Hot spots: Herring Cove Beach, Provincetown, 42.0461217 / -70.2185583; Race Point Beach, Provincetown, 42.0691855 / -70.2381706; Herring Pond, Eastham, 41.8230296 / -69.9879742; Corporation Beach, Dennis, 41.7517206 / -70.1874876; Mashpee Pond, Attaquin Park, Mashpee, 41.6515592 / -70.4834533

HORNED GREBE
Podiceps auritus

Easily defined in breeding season, this bird's white face and throat make it a dapper winter visitor as well.

Field marks: Breeding adult has rufous neck and sides; bright yellow, triangular patch on sides of head. Winter adult has short, whitish bill, black cap, white face, red eye, white neck, streaked sides, and black back.

Size: L: 13"–15", WS 18"

Similar species: Red-necked grebe is larger and drabber in winter. Eared grebe is smaller with a peaked head and very unusual on the Atlantic coast.

Season: Late fall, winter, early spring

Habitat: Open ocean, often viewable from shore

Food source: Insects, fish, small sea animals

Nest: On a rock or on floating plant matter in water

Call: Silent in winter; high, squeaky, descending laugh, ending in a series of low notes

Hot spots: Head of the Meadow Beach, North Truro, 42.0522244 / -70.0795126; Coast Guard Beach, Eastham, 41.8344618 / -69.9453163; Corporation Beach, Dennis, 41.7517206 / -70.1874876; Craigville Beach, Centerville, 41.6369994 / -70.3406954; Scusset Beach State Reservation, Sagamore Beach, 41.7781927 / -70.500555

WATERFOWL

MUTE SWAN
Cygnus olor
This introduced Eurasian species is expanding its numbers rapidly throughout the Northeast.

Field marks: All white bird, curved neck, orange bill with a black knob on top.

Size: L: 55"–61", WS: 84"–94"

Similar species: Tundra swan has a straight neck, black bill with yellow spot at its base. Trumpeter swan is larger and has an all-black bill.

Season: Year-round

Habitat: Freshwater lakes and marshes, saltwater bays

Food source: Aquatic plants

Nest: Mounds of grass and reeds not far from water

Call: Often silent, but can vocalize using hisses and short barks

Hot spots: Town Cove, Orleans, 41.787633 / -69.9854636; Frost Fish Creek, Chatham, 41.7017916 / -69.9701428; Bell's Neck Conservation Area, West Harwich, 41.6840342 / -70.1129007; Hallett's Millpond, Yarmouth, 41.7048154 / -70.2586627; Old Fish Hatchery and Nye Pond, East Sandwich, 41.7286493 / -70.4315861

CANADA GOOSE
Branta canadensis
You won't have to go far to find this ubiquitous bird.

Field marks: Brown body, lighter brown breast, black neck, black head with white band around throat and cheeks, gray bill, white vent.

Size: L: 25"–43" (considerable variation), WS: 75"

Similar species: Brant is smaller and lacks white panel on face. Greater white-fronted goose has a pink bill and legs, white patch on face at edge of bill, and is lighter colored overall. Cackling goose is smaller with a shorter neck and is not found on Cape Cod.

Season: Year-round

Habitat: Any body of water near grasses, open fields, or marshes

Food source: Grass, human crops (rice, corn)

Nest: A pile of sticks and grasses in a field or lawn near water

Call: *Honk-a-honk, honk-a-honk* when taking flight or communicating in a flock

Hot spots: Canada geese are often seen on man-made ponds in landscaped residential areas, in mall parking lots, near piers or harbors, or on any lake or pond in the wild. You will have no difficulty locating these birds any time of year.

BRANT
Branta bernicla
The dark head and neck, white collar, and small size differentiate this goose from others.

Field marks: Brown-black head, neck, and breast; white collar just below head, long neck, gray belly, dark wings, white rump and tail coverts, black legs.

Size: L: 22"–25", WS: 42"

Similar species: Canada goose is larger and has white patch on head. Cackling goose has white head patch as well and is not found on Cape Cod.

Season: Winter, early spring migration

Habitat: Marshes, usually along Cape Cod Bay or the Atlantic Ocean shore

Food source: Plants, especially grasses, sedges, and lichens

Nest: On the ground near the seashore or in grasslands

Call: A low *cron*, with some cackling chatter

Hot spots: Sandwich Harbor marshes, Sandwich, 41.7657903 / -70.4834962; Falmouth Heights, Cape and Islands Ocean Sanctuary, Falmouth, 41.543164 / -70.5992281; West Dennis Beach, Dennis, 41.65 / -70.189; North Chatham Landing, Chatham, 41.7050557 / -69.9474621; Corn Hill, Truro, 42.0061611 / -70.076766

WOOD DUCK
Aix sponsa

One of North America's most colorful ducks, with the male's facial markings and green cap particularly distinctive.

Field marks: Male has green cap with crest at back of head, dark face with white outlines, ruddy breast, yellow flanks, green back, long tail with rusty undertail coverts. Female has white oval around eye, gray head and back, brown to buff flanks with contrasting spots. Eclipse plumage: Male turns gray-brown with green cap, red eye, gray face with white streaks, whitish throat, green wash on back and wings, gray breast and flanks.

Size: L: 17"–20", WS: 30"

Similar species: Harlequin duck is dark blue overall, with a white spot on face and rusty flanks. Mallard male has a solid bright green head, pale back, and a shorter tail.

Season: Year-round, though easiest to see before and after breeding season

Habitat: Ponds and lakes sheltered by trees; wetlands with high grasses

Food source: Plants, insects, small aquatic animals, amphibians

Nest: In a tree cavity or nest box

Call: Female has a *whir-up, whir-up* repeated call; male has a high-pitched whistle.

Hot spots: Beech Forest, Provincetown, 42.0670802 / -70.1953679; Wellfleet Bay Wildlife Sanctuary, Wellfleet, 41.8825315 / -69.995712; Bell's Neck Conservation Area, West Harwich, 41.6840342 / -70.1129007; Pogorelc Sanctuary, Barnstable, 41.699604 / -70.355493; Mashpee Pond, Attaquin Park, Mashpee, 41.6515592 / -70.4834533

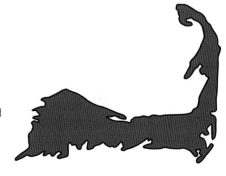

MALLARD
Anas platyrhynchos

The most common dabbling duck in the United States, the mallard is found in virtually every lake, pond, or large puddle.

Field marks: Male has green head, yellow bill, white collar, rusty breast, pale brown body, black and white tail. Female is uniformly brown with a paler head and black crown and line through the eye, orange bill with a dark center spot, blue speculum on wings with a white outline, and orange legs.

Size: L: 20"–26", WS: 35"

Similar species: American black duck is darker overall, with a lighter head and no wing speculum. Northern shoveler has much longer gray bill, a white breast, and rusty flanks. Ring-necked duck has navy blue head, gray bill with a white outline, and black back.

Season: Year-round

Habitat: Open water from small ponds and wetlands to large lakes, usually close to shore. Mallards also feed in grassy marshes and open land areas.

Food source: Insects, freshwater invertebrates, worms, seeds, crop leavings, aquatic plants

Nest: On the ground in grassland, marshes, and near lakes and ponds

Call: The stereotypical *quek, quek, quek*

Hot spots: Mallards can be found in or near any body of water in wild places or in coexistence with humans. Ponds in mall parking areas, housing developments, and schoolyards all host mallards, as do harbors, piers, and parks where people feed them (not a recommended practice).

AMERICAN BLACK DUCK
Anas rubripes
Find this dark-plumage dabbling duck in salt marshes and large ponds and lakes.

Field marks: Dark brown overall, with a somewhat lighter head and gray-streaked throat with a purple speculum with a black border. Female has a gray-green bill; male's bill is yellow.

Size: L: 22"–25", WS: 35"

Similar species: Female mallard is lighter overall, has an orange bill and legs, and has a white border around its blue speculum.

Season: Winter on the Outer Cape; winter through spring migration in the lower peninsula

Habitat: Salt marshes, ponds, lakes

Food source: Aquatic plants, seeds, insects, crustaceans, amphibians

Nest: Near water, on the ground or among tall grasses

Call: *Quack, quack*, but in a lower voice than a mallard

Hot spots: More common in the region than mallards, American black ducks stay together in small flocks and often disappear into reedy marshes, hidden by their muted plumage. Race Point Beach, Provincetown, 42.0691855 / -70.2381706; Great Island, Wellfleet, 41.9183734 / -70.0663376; Outermost Harbor, Chatham, 41.6649423 / -69.9501657; Hallett's Millpond, Yarmouth, 41.7048154 / -70.2586627; Great Sippewissett Marsh and Black Beach, Falmouth, 41.5890703 / -70.6442209

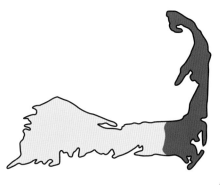

GREEN-WINGED TEAL
Anas crecca
America's smallest duck sports a bold facial pattern in breeding plumage.

Field marks: Breeding male has a rufous head with a green band from the eye to the back of the head, gray wings and flanks with a white bar on forward flank. Nonbreeding male is brown overall with visible green speculum. Female is mottled brown overall with a buff streak at the tail; green speculum is visible at rest.

Size: L: 12"–15", WS: 21"–25"

Similar species: Blue-winged teal has a blue head with a white crescent at the base of the bill, blue wing patch.

Season: Winter along the Atlantic coast; inland during spring and fall migration

Habitat: Lakes, ponds, and wetlands

Food source: Seeds, grasses, aquatic insects, small crustaceans

Nest: In a depression on the ground, some distance from water, in Canada and the northern United States west of New England

Call: Brief, staccato whistles from male; laughing *haw-haw* quack from female

Hot spots: Santuit Pond, Mashpee, 41.6552018 / -70.4597425; Bell's Neck Conservation Area, West Harwich, 41.6840342 / -70.1129007; Mill Pond, Barnstable, 41.7099896 / -70.3866148; Fort Hill, Eastham, 41.818792 / -69.9644995; High Head, Pilgrim Heights, Provincetown, 42.0563031 / -70.1161194

RING-NECKED DUCK
Aythya collaris
You'll have to look closely to find the reddish-brown "ring" around this duck's neck.

Field marks: Note the peaked back of the head. Dark purple head, yellow eye, gray bill with white ring and black tip, black back, light gray flanks with a white bar extending upward, black rear. Female is brown overall, with a white line through the eye, a white area just before the bill, and a gray bill with a black tip.

Size: L: 14"–18", WS: 24"–30"

Similar species: Greater scaup has a dark head with a greenish hue. Lesser scaup has a peaked head, no white on the bill, whiter sides, and a lighter back.

Season: Winter on the Upper Cape; an occasional winter sighting north of Eastham

Habitat: Freshwater ponds, marshes, bogs with considerable vegetation

Food source: Pondweed seeds and tubers, other aquatic plants, mollusks, waterborne insects and invertebrates

Nest: Among marsh plants, directly over water

Call: Brief whistled note from male; sharp, repeated *quack* from female

Hot spots: Herring Pond, Eastham, 41.8230296 / -69.9879742; Nickerson State Park, Brewster, 41.7540898 / -70.0206757; Bell's Neck Conservation Area, West Harwich, 41.6840342 / -70.1129007; Mill Pond, Barnstable, 41.7099896 / -70.3866148; Mashpee Pond, Attaquin Park, Mashpee, 41.6515592 / -70.4834533

GREATER SCAUP
Aythya marila
This steeply declining diving duck may be difficult to find among the more numerous lesser scaup.

Field marks: Round, dark head, appearing greenish in the right light (it can also appear dark blue or purple); yellow eye, light blue bill, gray back, white sides, dark rear. Female is uniformly brown with a gray bill and a white facial patch at base of bill.

Size: L: 17.5"–18", WS: 28"–30"

Similar species: Lesser scaup is smaller, has a dark blue head (though it can appear green), and its head comes to a point at the top rear.

Season: Winter along the coast; inland during spring and fall migration

Habitat: Ocean coastline in winter; lakes and bays during migration

Food source: Aquatic plants and seeds, mollusks, snails, small crustaceans, insects

Nest: On the ground in areas of tall grass, usually where water cannot reach it

Call: Descending *kuck-oo* from male; rapid, low *quack* from female

Hot spots: Race Point Beach, Provincetown, 42.0691855 / -70.2381706; High Head, Pilgrim Heights, Provincetown, 42.0563031 / -70.1161194; Herring Pond, Eastham, 41.8230296 / -69.9879742; Long Pond, Harwich, 41.719851 / -70.086099; Salt Pond, Falmouth, 41.542976 / -70.62774

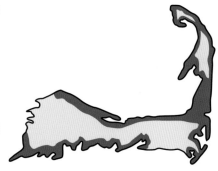

LESSER SCAUP
Aythya affinis
Look for large flocks of this diving duck during spring and fall migration.

Field marks: Dark head appears glossy navy blue in the right light; the pointed peak at the top rear is the best indication of a lesser (rather than greater) scaup. Yellow eye, gray bill, black breast and rear, gray back, white flanks. Female resembles the female greater scaup, but with a narrower white band at the base of the bill.

Size: L: 16"–18", WS: 24"–30"

Similar species: Greater scaup is slightly larger, with a rounded head (no peak) that may appear greenish in sunlight.

Season: Winter; spring and fall migration

Habitat: Lakes, bays, estuaries, reservoirs

Food source: Aquatic invertebrates

Nest: On the ground in areas of high grasses and sedges, on dry land or near lakes, generally in western United States prairies and marshes

Call: Male call a bubbly series of high-pitched *piffs*; female a hoarse, repeated *quick*

Hot spots: Mashpee Pond, Attaquin Park, Mashpee, 41.6515592 / -70.4834533; Wequaquet Lake, Barnstable, 41.6685842 / -70.3419399; Hinckleys Pond, Harwich, 41.7143786 / -70.0913572; Town Cove, Orleans, 41.787633 / -69.9854636; Great Pond, Eastham, 41.8339501 / -69.9896908

COMMON EIDER
Somateria mollissima

This striking diving duck is a New England specialty, lingering in harbors and inland bays in all seasons. Of the four varieties of common eider that live in North America, the local population is the Atlantic (*dresseri*) variety.

Field marks: Pie slice–shaped head with black cap, white face, steeply sloping forehead, olive greenish bill, white back, black flanks and underparts, black tail. Female is cinnamon brown with a gray bill, barred throughout the back and flanks.

Size: L: 24"–27", WS: 36"–40"

Similar species: King eider is smaller and has a gray-blue hood and distinctive yellow and orange bill.

Season: Year-round, with larger concentrations in winter

Habitat: Open ocean, saltwater bays and harbors

Food source: Shellfish

Nest: On the ground near water

Call: Male and female call a raspy, continuous *kor-kor-kor;* male also calls a rising *wha-woo.*

Hot spots: MacMillan Wharf, Provincetown, 42.0494838 / -70.181694; Sandy Neck Beach, Barnstable, 41.7391369 / -70.3801775; Kalmus Park Beach, Hyannis, 41.6345887 / -70.2768735; Monomoy National Wildlife Refuge, Morris Island, Chatham, 41.6568485 / -69.9582152; Sandwich Marina, Sandwich, 41.7736623 / -70.4996526

LONG-TAILED DUCK
Clangula hyemalis
The tail of this luxuriously plumaged diving duck makes it one of a kind in Cape Cod waters.

Field marks: Winter male has white cap, gray face, black bill with bright pink stripe, black spot between head and neck, white neck and breast, white cape of feathers across back, black and brown flanks, dark wings, white rump, long black tail curling or pointing upward. Female has white head with black smudge, greenish bill, chestnut brown body, white rump, short tail.

Size: L: 16"–22", WS: 26"–30"

Similar species: Northern pintail has a long neck, brown face, dark gray bill.

Season: Winter

Habitat: A variety of ocean inlets (bays, harbors, etc.) near shore

Food source: Invertebrates found near the surface or at the bottom of the ocean

Nest: On the ground near water in northern Canada

Call: Male call is *oh, oh-a-doo-a-lee*; female is *git, git, git.*

Hot spots: Sandy Neck Beach, Barnstable, 41.7391369 / -70.3801775; Falmouth Harbor, Falmouth, 41.5461351 / -70.6036806; Nauset Beach, Orleans, 41.7888489 / -69.9355316; Chatham Light and Lighthouse Beach, Chatham, 41.6714212 / -69.9490499; Race Point Beach, Provincetown, 42.0691855 / -70.2381706

SURF SCOTER
Melanitta perspicillata
Watch rafts of scoters for this diving duck's orange and white bill.

Field marks: Male has a black body and head, white patch on back of head, bright orange and white bill with a black spot on each side. Female is uniformly dark brown with a black cap, a white facial patch, and a white patch before the bill.

Size: L: 17"–21", WS: 30"–34"

Similar species: Black scoter lacks white head patch and orange on bill. White-winged scoter is browner, with a white wing patch.

Season: Winter

Habitat: Atlantic and Cape Cod Bay coastlines

Food source: Small fish, mollusks, crustaceans, water insects, underwater plants

Nest: In the Arctic from Alaska to northern Labrador

Call: A squeaky *buk, buk*, often with wing sounds; soft, repetitive *whudda-whudda-whudda*

Hot spots: Race Point, Provincetown, 42.0691855 / -70.2381706; Head of the Meadow Beach, North Truro, 42.0522244 / -70.0795126; Nauset Light Beach, Eastham, 41.8586304 / -69.9517322; Monomoy National Wildlife Refuge, Chatham, 41.6568485 / -69.9582152; Long Pasture Wildlife Sanctuary, Barnstable, 41.70703 / -70.27171

BLACK SCOTER
Melanitta nigra
The darkest scoter overall, with a smaller, flashy yellow bill, this diving duck prefers salt water almost exclusively in winter.

Field marks: Male has black head and body, bill with bright yellow knob and grayish tip. Female is dark brown with a white cheek patch and light area before the bill.

Size: L: 17"–20", WS: 30"–34"

Similar species: Surf scoter has white head patch and orange on the bill. White-winged scoter has white wing patch, white crescent below the eye, and is browner overall.

Season: Winter

Habitat: Oceans and large saltwater bays

Food source: Mollusks, small fish, crustaceans, algae, underwater plants

Nest: Disguised in a crack between rocks or behind a grass hummock; the Arctic from Alaska to Labrador

Call: Descending whistle: *peeuu, peeuu,* on the water or in flight

Hot spots: Herring Cove Beach, Provincetown, 42.0461217 / -70.2185583; Highland Light area, Province-town, 42.0393753 / -70.0621842; Chatham Light and Lighthouse Beach, Chatham, 41.6714212 / -69.9490499; Hyannis-Nantucket ferry, departing from Hyannis Harbor, 41.6463678 / -70.2747006; Scusset Beach State Reserva-tion, Sagamore Beach, 41.7781927 / -70.500555

WHITE-WINGED SCOTER
Melanitta fusca
The largest of the local scoters is easy to pick out in flight, thanks to its namesake wing patch.

Field marks: Male has dark brown body and head, orange bill with a gray knob and tip, white crescent under the eye, white wing patch. Female is lighter brown with a black cap, two white patches on the head, and white wing patch.

Size: L: 19"–24", WS: 33"–40"

Similar species: Black scoter and surf scoter lack the white wing patch and eye crescent.

Season: Winter

Habitat: Open ocean and coastal bays in winter

Food source: Mollusks, small fish, crustaceans, water insects, underwater plants

Nest: On the ground in a crevice near water; Alaska and northern Canada

Call: A soft, single *churp*. A flock will chatter continuously during takeoff.

Hot spots: Race Point, Provincetown, 42.0691855 / -70.238170; Head of the Meadow Beach, North Truro, 42.0522244 / -70.0795126; Nauset Light Beach, Eastham, 41.8586304 / -69.9517322; Sandy Neck Beach, Barnstable, 41.7391369 / -70.3801775; Hyannis-Nantucket ferry, departing from Hyannis Harbor, 41.6463678 / -70.2747006

COMMON GOLDENEYE
Bucephala clangula
A winter resident through most of the region, this diving duck prefers coastal waters.

Field marks: Male has dark green head, "golden" yellow eye, round white cheek patch, white flanks, black and white back with thin black barring over white, black rear end. Female has brown head, mostly black bill with yellow tip, gray body and wings, white wing patch.

Size: L: 17"–20", WS: 25"–30"

Similar species: Barrow's goldeneye has a flatter head and more defined black barring on back, with a black leading line at the shoulder.

Season: Winter

Habitat: Ocean bays, estuaries, inlets, lakes

Food source: Mollusks, crustaceans, water insects, small fish, plants in waterways

Nest: In tree cavities in Canada and northern Maine, usually near a lake or pond

Call: A high *jip-jeet* or a guttural grunt, accompanied by wing whistles in flight

Hot spots: Dowses Beach, Osterville, 41.6221797 / -70.3663588; Ashumet Pond, Mashpee, 41.6325966 / -70.5341578; Long Pond, Harwich, 41.719851 / -70.086099; Town Cove, Orleans, 41.787633 / -69.9854636; Corn Hill, Truro, 42.0061611 / -70.076766

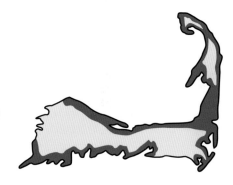

BUFFLEHEAD
Bucephala albeola
North America's smallest diving duck overwinters in ponds, lakes, and bays along the New England coast.

Field marks: Male has large white area on back of the black head, small bill, black back, white flanks and underside, gray tail. Nonbreeding male loses much of the white area on the head, retaining a patch on each side. Female is all brown with a darker back and head, white oval patch on each side of the head.

Size: L: 13"–14", WS: 21"–24"

Similar species: Hooded merganser is much larger and has a thin black bill, as well as rusty flanks and distinctive white striping.

Season: Winter on the coast; spring and fall migration farther inland

Habitat: Ponds, lakes, inlets, some open ocean

Food source: Insects, mollusks, crustaceans, some seeds found underwater

Nest: In cavities, often those left behind by northern flickers

Call: A single syllable *quah*, or a continuous *qua-qua-qua* during breeding season

Hot spots: Widespread and numerous, buffleheads crowd together in flocks along the Atlantic Ocean and on Cape Cod Bay in winter, moving to inland lakes, ponds, and inlets in the shoulder seasons. Any coastal overlook, quiet wharf, or active harbor may host these small ducks.

COMMON MERGANSER
Mergus merganser
Look for the largest of the mergansers on inland lakes, rivers, and ponds.

Field marks: Male in breeding plumage has dark greenish-black head, very thin red bill, white breast and flanks, black back, and gray rear. Female is drabber, with a tousled reddish-brown head, white throat and top of breast, and gray body overall. Male in nonbreeding plumage resembles female, with a subtle crest and a white wing patch.

Size: L: 24"–27", WS: 32"–36"

Similar species: Male red-breasted merganser has a tousled crest, white band around the neck, and gray flanks.

Season: Winter

Habitat: Lakes, rivers, ocean bays and inlets

Food source: Small fish, insects, underwater plants

Nest: In a hollow tree or a deep depression on the ground

Call: An insect-like *crkkkk* from the male; a low, repeated *crak-crak-crak* from the female

Hot spots: High Head, Pilgrim Heights, Provincetown, 42.0563031 / -70.1161194; Great Pond, Eastham, 41.8339501 / -69.9896908; Long Pond, Harwich, 41.719851 / -70.086099; Shubael Pond, Marstons Mills, 41.67413 / -70.394693; Santuit Pond, Mashpee, 41.6552018 / -70.4597425

RED-BREASTED MERGANSER
Mergus serrator
The duck with the ragged crest and long, red bill turns up at every coastal pond and inlet in winter, spring, and fall.

Field marks: Male has dark greenish-black head, ragged crest, long red bill, white collar, reddish-brown breast, black and white back, gray flanks. Female and nonbreeding male are virtually identical, with reddish-brown heads and gray bodies.

Size: L: 20"–26", WS: 30"–34"

Similar species: Common merganser lacks the tousled crest and reddish breast. Hooded merganser has a large white patch on the neatly shaped crest.

Season: Spring and fall migration; winter along the coast

Habitat: Year-round in waters around the Outer Cape; winter, spring and fall migration on Cape Cod Bay and on inland lakes and ponds

Food source: Primarily fish, but will eat water insects, worms, small amphibians, and crustaceans

Nest: In a hidden hole in the ground or a brush pile; the North Country from the Great Lakes to Alaska

Call: A soft *wuh, wuh-wuh* from the male; a quacking call from the female

Hot spots: No scan of the winter coastline is complete until you've tallied at least a couple pairs of red-breasted mergansers, often associating with common mergansers and other diving ducks. If you do not spot them immediately from the beach, try small lakes and ponds farther inland, where they may congregate as weather begins to warm toward spring.

DOUBLE-CRESTED CORMORANT
Phalacrocorax auritus
Very common large, black seabird on ocean shores and large freshwater lakes.

Field marks: Black overall; orange lores, gray bill; white tufts on crown during breeding. Juveniles have pale or tan throat and underside.

Size: L: 32"–33", WS: 50"–54"

Similar species: Great cormorant is larger and has a white throat.

Season: Year-round

Habitat: Open water, especially along the ocean shore, but also found inland at large lakes and flowing rivers.

Food source: Fish, crustaceans

Nest: In rocky or sandy areas along ocean, lake, or river shoreline

Call: Mostly silent; some grunting during nesting

Hot spots: Virtually every beach wall, rocky outcropping, offshore island, and sandbar along the Atlantic coast has its own complement of double-crested cormorants, and many large inland lakes and reservoirs provide homes to these large, dark birds as well. You do not need a special hot spot to find one—just go to any beach or shoreline overlook and scan the horizon. Cormorants sit low in the water, making them look similar to loons, so check carefully for the bright orange-yellow bill to make the identification.

GULLS AND TERNS

LAUGHING GULL
Leucophaeus atricilla

Named for its cackling call, this black-headed gull is one of the most widespread gull species on Cape Cod.

Field marks: Breeding adult has black head extending to the neck, partial white eye ring, heavy red bill that droops slightly at the end; white body, dark wings, white tail with black band at the end, black legs. Nonbreeding adult has white head streaked in gray at the back, black bill.

Size: L: 16"–17", WS: 40"–42"

Similar species: Little gull is smaller, has a slim bill, and has a dark underwing. Bonaparte's gull is smaller and has a thin black bill and light gray wings.

Season: Spring through fall; some individuals overwinter along the coastline.

Habitat: Ocean beaches, salt marshes

Food source: Insects and invertebrates, shellfish, berries, human trash

Nest: On the ground in a salt marsh, hidden among grasses

Call: Repeated *kyah, kyah*, increasing in speed until it sounds like a human laugh

Hot spots: Laughing gulls are prevalent from Sandwich to Provincetown, with numbers increasing through the fall as more northerly gulls pass through during their migration south. Rarely straying inland, they congregate on beaches and around the edges of bays, foraging in flocks and often coming within a few feet of humans. Any visit to a beach in summer will reveal these gulls standing on fence posts, strutting on boardwalk railings, and poking around changing and restroom facilities.

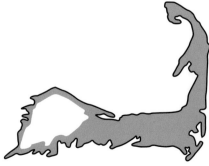

RING-BILLED GULL
Larus delawarensis
The most common gull in America, this scavenger turns up in flocks in parking lots, in mowed grassy areas, and at your outdoor restaurant table.

Field marks: Breeding adult has white head and body; yellow bill with black ring near the tip, gray wings, black wing tips, yellow legs. Juveniles have varying degrees of brown streaking over the head, body, and wings; pink bill with black tip, pink legs.

Size: L: 17.5"–19", WS: 47"–48"

Similar species: Herring gull is larger and has a yellow bill with a red spot. Laughing gull has a black hood in breeding season, and has darker wings year-round.

Season: Year-round resident

Habitat: Ocean beaches, lagoons, inlets, marshes, parks, parking lots, landfills

Food source: Human discards, fish, rodents, eggs and chicks from other birds' nests

Nest: In a depression on the ground; in colonies on an island or other protected area

Call: Piercing *keey-oh, keey-oh*, or a harsh, high-pitched barking call

Hot spots: You will see these ubiquitous birds every time you visit the beach, go to a supermarket or park, or venture into any wilderness area that contains a lake or large pond.

HERRING GULL
Larus argentatus
The number of plumage variations for this common gull can drive a birder to distraction.

Field marks: Breeding adult has white head and breast, yellow eye, heavy yellow bill with red spot on lower mandible; gray wings with black tips, white tail, pink legs. Nonbreeding adult is similar but with brown streaking on the head and neck. Juveniles in first and second winter have extensive brown mottling over the head, breast, underside, tail, and wings, with black wing tips and a dark brown band at the end of the tail. Extent of streaking will vary from one bird to the next.

Size: L: 24"–26", WS: 55"–58"

Similar species: Great black-backed gull is larger and has black wings. Lesser black-backed gull is slightly smaller and has darker gray wings and yellow legs. Ring-billed gull is smaller and has a yellow bill with a black ring.

Season: Year-round

Habitat: Ocean beaches, islands, large lakes, rivers

Food source: Fish, aquatic invertebrates, shellfish, carrion, other birds, human discards

Nest: On the ground on the beach or an island not far from shore

Call: A squeal followed by a high *hyah-hyah-hyah-hyah*, not unlike a human laugh. Other calls include a long whistle ending in a high-pitched squeal.

Hot spots: Find these gulls on any open beach, as well as in the beach parking areas, the adjacent wetlands, and along the shores of large lakes or riverbanks. You may also find them feeding on and around landfills.

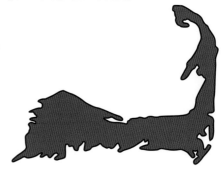

GREAT BLACK-BACKED GULL
Larus marinus
The largest local gull stands out from a mixed flock because of its height and true-black wings.

Field marks: Adult has white head and body, yellow bill with red spot on lower mandible, black wings with large white spots on primaries, pinkish legs. Juvenile has darkly streaked head and body, mottled black and white wings, large black bill, pale pink legs. Streaking fades over the course of three winters.

Size: L: 28"–31", WS: 62"–65"

Similar species: Lesser black-backed gull is smaller with yellow legs; wings are dark gray rather than black. Herring gull is smaller and has gray wings.

Season: Year-round

Habitat: Ocean coast, tidal wetlands, bays and inlets

Food source: An aggressive scavenger: fish, mollusks, crustaceans, small mammals, insects, bird eggs and chicks, berries, human discards

Nest: Tucked in among rocks on a cliff face or other rocky outcropping

Call: Deeper-throated than other gulls; an alto moan, leading to a series of *ay-yah, ay-yah, ay-yah* syllables in various combinations

Hot spots: You'll find these large gulls among flocks of ring-billed, herring, and laughing gulls on virtually every beach, as well as on large lakes, inlets, and even on mudflats in salt marshes. With their black backs and wings, bright yellow bills, and several inches more height than the gulls around them, great black-backs make it fairly easy to sort them out from the crowd of gray-winged varieties.

COMMON TERN
Sterna hirundo

Small, slender, and strong with a forked tail like a barn swallow, this is New England's most numerous tern.

Field marks: Breeding adult has a white head, light gray body, black cap that narrows toward the back of the neck, red bill with black tip, pale gray wings that extend past the tail, deeply forked tail, dark primaries visible on underwing, red legs. Nonbreeding adult has black cap on back of head, exposing white forehead; black bill, dark "shoulder" on wing, black legs. Juvenile birds have gray wings streaked with white, limited black cap with white forehead, black bill and legs.

Size: L: 12"–15", WS: 30"–31"

Similar species: Arctic tern is smaller with very short, red legs and a short bill. Tail of Forster's tern extends past the wings. Roseate tern has a black bill and a long tail.

Season: Spring through fall

Habitat: Beaches, inlets and bays with rocky shorelines

Food source: Fish, mollusks, squid, crustaceans, some insects

Nest: On the ground on a beach, in seaweed or gravel just above the high-tide line

Call: A gravelly *kee-yur*; a single chip note in flight

Hot spots: Flocks of terns commandeer stretches of beach and stand in rows, while others flash past over bays and ocean waters, searching for their next meal. Any beach will yield sightings of these birds from May through September, with continued streams of migrants through November. It is not uncommon to see hundreds or even thousands of common terns while standing on a beach in August or September as migration gets under way.

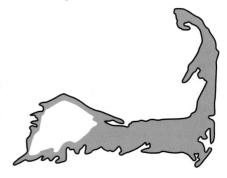

LEAST TERN
Sternula antillarum
Cape Cod's smallest tern is distinctive, with its aggressive diving style, white forehead, and yellow bill.

Field marks: Breeding adult has white head and body, black cap, white forehead, yellow bill, pale gray wings, two dark gray primaries, white tail with short V shape, yellow legs. Nonbreeding bird has black bill, light primaries; black cap recedes to middle of head.

Size: L: 8"–9", WS: 20"

Similar species: All other terns are larger; only least tern has a yellow bill and legs.

Season: Spring through fall

Habitat: Sandy beaches and sandbars

Food source: Fish, shrimp

Nest: In the sand on a beach

Call: Single, repeated note: *chik, chik, chik*; faster and squeakier when used as an alarm

Hot spots: Just about any beach may host least terns throughout the summer. These are particularly reliable: Head of the Meadow Beach, North Truro, 42.0522244 / -70.0795126; Nauset Beach, Orleans, 41.7888489 / -69.9355316; Forest Beach and Conservation Lands, Chatham, 41.6700588 / -70.0253749; Chapin Beach, Dennis, 41.730314 / -70.2350271; South Cape Beach State Park, Mashpee, 41.5536361 / -70.4993146

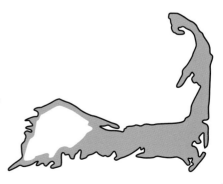

HERONS AND EGRETS

GREAT BLUE HERON
Ardea herodias

The tallest of the long-legged waders, this majestic bird stands quietly and waits for prey, then grabs or stabs its target in a split-second attack.

Field marks: Gray-blue with grayish legs, large bill, yellow lower mandible, black crown, long plumes from neck. In flight, legs extend far beyond tail, neck curls in, and darker flight feathers become visible.

Size: H: 46", WS: 72"

Similar species: Tricolored heron has white underbelly. Little blue heron is darker blue and half as tall.

Season: Year-round wherever there is open water

Habitat: Fresh- and saltwater marshes, grasslands, any pond with ample fish

Food source: Fish, small mammals, frogs, birds, insects

Nest: High in trees in colonies (rookeries), often some distance from feeding grounds

Call: Hoarse croaking *bwaaaaah*; alarm is a series of chuffing sounds like *bwaak, bwaak, bwaak.*

Hot spots: The most common tall wading bird in America, the great blue heron can be seen easily at virtually any inland pond, tidal marsh, and wetland wildlife refuge on the Cape.

GREAT EGRET

Ardea alba

Cape Cod's tallest egret is a sight to behold. Pure white with a long, curving neck, it's easy to see as it stands motionless and waits for prey to swim by.

Field marks: All white, long yellow-orange bill, black legs and feet.

Size: H: 39", WS: 51"

Similar species: Snowy egret has a black bill with yellow lores, black legs, and yellow feet.

Season: Spring through fall

Habitat: Salt- and freshwater marshes, mudflats, other wetlands along the coasts

Food source: Fish, frogs, other small wetland creatures

Nest: In colonies, high in trees

Call: Low, squawking *caaaah*, dropping still lower at the end

Hot spots: Wellfleet Bay Wildlife Sanctuary, Wellfleet, 41.8825315 / -69.995712; Nauset Marsh, Eastham, 41.8143142 / -69.9504232; Monomoy National Wildlife Refuge, Morris Island, Chatham, 41.6568485 / -69.9582152; Pogorelc Sanctuary, Barnstable, 41.699604 / -70.355493; Hallett's Millpond, Yarmouth, 41.7048154 / -70.2586627

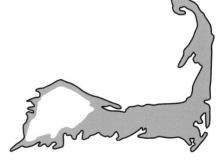

SNOWY EGRET
Egretta thula

This elegant member of the heron family sports long plumes during the breeding season; its bright yellow feet make it unique among egrets.

Field marks: All white; long white plumes from head and chest during breeding season, slender black bill, yellow lores, black legs with yellow feet.

Size: H: 24", WS: 41"

Similar species: Great egret is significantly larger and has a yellow-orange bill and black feet. Cattle egret is smaller and has shorter, orange-red bill and black feet (red during breeding).

Season: Spring and fall migration; summer in coastal marshes

Habitat: Marshes (salt, brackish, and freshwater), ponds, wetlands

Food source: Fish, small crustaceans, worms, frogs, insects

Nest: In colonies, toward the tops of trees or tall shrubs

Call: Croaking *maaaw, morr*; higher pitched than great egret or great blue heron

Hot spots: Wellfleet Bay Wildlife Sanctuary, Wellfleet, 41.8825315 / -69.995712; First Encounter Beach, Eastham, 41.8215025 / -70.0037241; Fort Hill, Eastham, 41.818792 / -69.9644995; Buck's Creek, Chatham, 41.673952 / -70.0011545; Pogorelc Sanctuary, Barnstable, 41.699604 / -70.355493

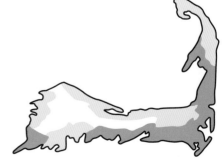

GREEN HERON
Butorides virescens

A quiet, secretive hunter, the green heron moves slowly among tall grasses at the edges of estuaries or ponds and waits for prey to reveal itself.

Field marks: Dark green back, chestnut neck and head, dark crest, long dark bill, yellow legs. Often seen hunkered down on the edge of a creek or riverbank, then standing with neck extended to full length. Young birds have white streaks on chestnut neck.

Size: H: 18", WS: 26"

Similar species: Night-herons are white, gray, and black, with no chestnut or green areas. American bittern is a lighter brown overall, though neck is similarly streaked. Least bittern is a similar size, but has bright yellow-brown plumage.

Season: Spring through fall

Habitat: Banks of creeks, ponds, and rivers; usually seen low and close to the water

Food source: Primarily fish

Nest: Hidden in a tree from ground level to 30 feet up, usually (but not always) near a water source

Call: A low, throaty *ga-wuh*; a surprisingly high *kyur* alarm call or a chattering *kuh-kuh-kuh* when something gets too close to the nest

Hot spots: High Head, Pilgrim Heights, Provincetown, 42.0563031 / -70.1161194; Wellfleet Bay Wildlife Sanctuary, Wellfleet, 41.8825315 / -69.995712; Cape Cod National Seashore, Salt Pond Visitor Center, Eastham, 41.837154 / -69.9726588; Pogorelc Sanctuary, Barnstable, 41.699604 / -70.355493; South Cape Beach State Park, Mashpee, 41.5536361 / -70.4993146

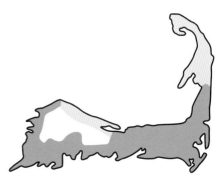

PLOVERS

BLACK-BELLIED PLOVER
Pluvialis squatarola

The region's largest plover is easy to spot, with its black face, neck, breast, and underside in breeding plumage.

Field marks: Breeding adult has white head with grayish cap; black face, breast, and underside; short black bill, white undertail coverts, mottled gray and white mantle, black legs; black "armpits" visible in flight. Nonbreeding bird has gray head and breast, light gray to white underside, mottled gray mantle.

Size: L: 11.5"–13", WS: 25"–29"

Similar species: American golden plover has black undertail coverts, warm "golden" tan tone on back and wings.

Season: Spring and fall migration

Habitat: Wetland mudflats, open fields and pastures with standing water and muddy areas

Food source: Small invertebrates

Nest: On open tundra in Canada's Arctic region

Call: High-pitched whistled *peeu, peeu-ee*

Hot spots: Nauset Beach, Orleans, 41.7888489 / -69.9355316; Cowyard Lane, Chatham, 41.6957955 / -69.9512064; Callery Darling Conservation Area, Yarmouth, 41.7198563 / -70.2277851; Long Pasture Wildlife Sanctuary, Barnstable, 41.70703 / -70.27171; Great Sippewissett Marsh and Black Beach, Falmouth, 41.5890703 / -70.6442209

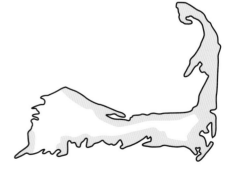

PIPING PLOVER
Charadrius melodus

This sand-colored bird earned its endangered species status by laying its eggs in a scrape on sandy beaches, making it especially vulnerable to human disturbance.

Field marks: Pale tan and white head with black stripe on forehead, orange bill with black tip, narrow black collar, pale tan back and wings, white underside, yellow legs. Nonbreeding bird has a black bill and a pale tan collar.

Size: L: 7.25", WS: 19"

Similar species: Semipalmated plover is darker brown, with a black mask and white forehead.

Season: Summer

Habitat: Ocean beach

Food source: Insects, small invertebrates

Nest: In a scrape of sand on ocean beach

Call: Low, whistled, elongated *ooo-ee, ooo-ee*, plus tiny, piping *peep* notes

Hot spots: Many beaches along the Atlantic coast provide protected breeding grounds for piping plovers. Watch for signs at beach entrances about protecting the plover during breeding season. Great Island, Wellfleet, 41.9183734 / -70.0663376; Coast Guard Beach, Eastham, 41.8344618 / -69.9453163; Nauset Beach, Orleans, 41.7888489 / -69.9355316; Monomoy National Wildlife Refuge, South Beach, Chatham, 41.6298145 / -69.9609375; East Sandwich Beach, Sandwich, 41.7527759 / -70.4425971

SEMIPALMATED PLOVER
Charadrius semipalmatus

"Semi-palms" are numerous in mixed flocks of migrating shorebirds; their bold facial pattern makes them easy to distinguish.

Field marks: Tan cap, black mask, white forehead and throat, yellow bill with black tip, black collar, tan back and wings, white underside, yellow legs. Nonbreeding bird has less-pronounced mask; bill is black on top and yellow below.

Size: L: 7.25", WS: 19"

Similar species: Piping plover is much lighter overall and lacks the dark mask. Killdeer is larger and has two wide black rings around its neck.

Season: Spring and fall migration, with much larger concentrations in fall

Habitat: Ocean beaches, muddy areas in open fields

Food source: Small invertebrates, insect larvae, tiny shellfish

Nest: In a low spot on the ground in the Canadian Arctic region

Call: A whistled *chee-up, chee-up*

Hot spots: Herring Cove Beach, Provincetown, 42.0461217 / -70.2185583; High Head, Pilgrim Heights, Provincetown, 42.0563031 / -70.1161194; Great Island, Wellfleet, 41.9183734 / -70.0663376; Coast Guard Beach, Eastham, 41.8344618 / -69.9453163; Tern Island Sanctuary, Chatham, 41.69068 / -69.947269

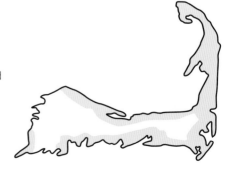

KILLDEER
Pluvialis vociferus

Nesting on golf courses, on beaches, in parking lots, and in other human-populated areas, the killdeer feigns a broken wing to lure potential predators away from its nest.

Field marks: Brown or rufous cap, white face with bold markings, two wide black rings across the throat and breast, rufous-brown back and wings, white underside, bright rufous rump; wide, white stripe the length of the wings visible in flight.

Size: L: 9"–10.5", WS: 20"–24"

Similar species: Semipalmated plover is smaller, has a yellow bill, and has only one ring around its neck.

Season: Spring through fall

Habitat: Large mowed lawns, golf courses, open prairie, farm fields

Food source: Insects and small invertebrates, especially worms and grasshoppers

Nest: In an area with gravel—a field, parking lot, golf course, or roof

Call: A piercing, repeated *kill-DEER, kill-DEER*

Hot spots: Birders who are used to spotting dozens of killdeer on trips may be surprised at how comparatively scarce these birds are on Cape Cod. These areas usually yield two or more in season: Bell's Neck Conservation Area, West Harwich, 41.6840342 / -70.1129007; Breivogel Ponds, Falmouth, 41.6066506 / -70.5907631; West Dennis Beach, Dennis, 41.65 / -70.189; Wellfleet Bay Wildlife Sanctuary, Wellfleet, 41.8825315 / -69.995712; Race Point, Provincetown, 42.0691855 / -70.2381706

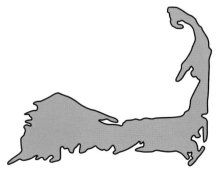

OYSTERCATCHER

AMERICAN OYSTERCATCHER

Haematopus palliatus

With its clownish features and propensity for chatter, the local oystercatcher makes itself unmistakable on local beaches.

Field marks: Black head and neck, orange eye and long orange bill, white chest and underside, brown back and wings, white stripe on wings visible in flight, white rump, pale yellow legs.

Size: L: 17"–21", WS: 32"

Similar species: Black skimmer has a more tapered body, a black back and wings, and a two-toned orange and black bill with a longer lower mandible.

Season: Summer, fall migration

Habitat: Ocean beaches

Food source: A variety of shellfish, including oysters

Nest: In a scrape in the sand on ocean beaches

Call: A variety of hurried *peeps*, sung in quick succession; also short, single *peep*, longer *pee-uy* calls in flight

Hot spots: Most beaches and areas with exposed mudflats attract a pair or two of oystercatchers in summer, and several individuals during fall migration. These hot spots offer the most consistent sightings: Wellfleet Bay Wildlife Sanctuary, Wellfleet, 41.8825315 / -69.995712; Monomoy National Wildlife Refuge, Chatham, 41.5913346 / -69.9880211; Jeremy Point, Wellfleet, 41.878061 / -70.0673676; Nauset Marsh, Eastham, 41.8143142 / -69.9504232; Chapin Beach, Dennis, 41.730314 / -70.2350271

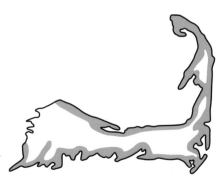

SANDPIPERS AND SNIPE

RUDDY TURNSTONE
Arenaria interpres

This boldly patterned member of the sandpiper family stands out from the crowd on beaches and mudflats.

Field marks: Breeding adult has striking black and white facial and breast pattern, russet back with wide white stripe up the middle; russet, black, and white wings; white rump, black end of tail, orange legs. Nonbreeding plumage is mottled gray and brown with a muted breast and head pattern. White underside in all seasons.

Size: L: 9"–10", WS: 18"–21"

Similar species: Killdeer is taller and thinner and has two wide black bands around the neck.

Season: Spring and fall migration

Habitat: Coastal beaches and mudflats

Food source: Mainly insects; some mollusks and crustaceans

Nest: In a hollow on the ground, in northern Canada and the Arctic region

Call: A rapid *week-a-teek-a-tee-tee-tee-tee*; abbreviated during feeding

Hot spots: Wellfleet Bay Wildlife Sanctuary, Wellfleet, 41.8825315 / -69.995712; Nauset Marsh, Eastham, 41.8143142 / -69.9504232; Monomoy National Wildlife Refuge, Chatham, 41.6568485 / -69.9582152; Corporation Beach, Dennis, 41.7517206 / -70.1874876; Dowses Beach, Osterville, 41.6221797 / -70.3663588

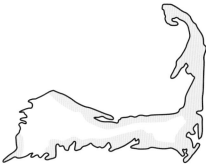

39

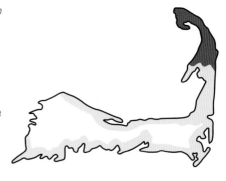

SANDERLING
Calidris alba

Easy to identify as they run back and forth on beaches just above the waves, these birds often move in large flocks.

Field marks: Breeding adult has reddish head and neck, short black bill, white underside, scaled black and brown wings, black legs; white wing stripe visible in flight. Nonbreeding bird is pale gray above, white below, with black bill and legs.

Size: L: 8", WS: 15"–17"

Similar species: Least and semipalmated sandpipers are smaller and lack the reddish breeding plumage. Least sandpiper has greenish legs in all seasons.

Season: Year-round north of Wellfleet; spring and fall migration on most shores

Habitat: Ocean beaches, tidal mudflats

Food source: Invertebrates, occasional insects

Nest: In a depression in the ground, on tundra in the Arctic region

Call: Whistling chatter or high-pitched *wip-wip-wip-wip*

Hot spots: No beach is complete without its flock of sanderlings, whether they form a single family unit or number in the hundreds. If you visit any of the Atlantic Ocean beaches in fall and winter, you will see these birds running up the beach as they avoid the incoming surf, and then dashing down it in remarkable unison to partake of whatever the tide brought in. Their distinctive plumage and regimented behavior helps differentiate them from other small sandpipers.

DUNLIN
Calidris alpina

The downward-curving bill and black belly patch in breeding plumage make this bird fairly easy to pick out of a group.

Field marks: Breeding adult has gray head, white breast with gray streaks, downward-curving bill, rufous back, scaly rufous and black wings, black patch on white belly, gray tail with white outer feathers, black legs. Nonbreeding bird has light brown head, grayish-brown back and wings, white underside.

Size: L: 7.5"–8.5", WS: 15"–17"

Similar species: Least and semipalmated sandpipers are smaller, have no rufous coloring, and lack the belly patch. Purple sandpiper is uniformly gray in winter and has yellow legs.

Season: Spring and fall migration; some winter flocks on beaches

Habitat: Ocean beaches, tidal mudflats, wetlands, lakeshores, riverbanks

Food source: Insects, aquatic invertebrates, snails, small crustaceans

Nest: On a dry, raised spot in open tundra; Arctic Canada and northern and coastal Alaska

Call: An elongated, scream-like *churr-eeeeee-errr*, rising in the middle

Hot spots: Check your local beach or your favorite mudflat in October and November before venturing farther to find this bird. If your local spot doesn't yield dunlins, try one of these refuges: Great Island, Wellfleet, 41.9183734 / -70.0663376; Nauset Beach, Orleans, 41.7888489 / -69.9355316; Monomoy National Wildlife Refuge, South Beach, Chatham, 41.6298145 / -69.9609375; Corporation Beach, Dennis, 41.7517206 / -70.1874876; Long Pasture Wildlife Sanctuary, Barnstable, 41.70703 / -70.27171

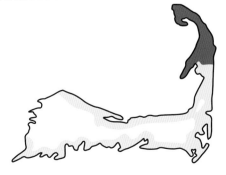

LEAST SANDPIPER
Calidris minutilla

Cape Cod's smallest sandpiper provides a simple way to tell it apart from others in its class: its yellowish legs.

Field marks: Breeding adult has brown head, chest, back and wings, with black scales over the brown on wings; small bill that droops down slightly at the end, white underside, yellow-green legs. Nonbreeding bird is gray instead of brown, but with a brownish head.

Size: L: 6", WS: 12"–13"

Similar species: Semipalmated sandpiper is slightly larger, has a straight bill and black legs. Western sandpiper is more rufous on head and back and has a longer bill and black legs.

Season: Spring and fall migration; summer on the Outer Cape

Habitat: Ocean and lake beaches, tidal mudflats

Food source: Small invertebrates, insects, some plant seeds

Nest: In a hollow on the ground, in northern Canada

Call: A high trill, interspersed with a *cheep* or *chirreep*

Hot spots: Least sandpipers are widespread and numerous during spring and fall migration, so you may see them on any beach or mudflat throughout late April and May, and again from August through September. The following hot spots provide locations where larger flocks collect: High Head, Pilgrim Heights, Provincetown, 42.0563031 / -70.1161194; Lieutenant Island and Causeway, Wellfleet, 41.8960801 / -70.0161266; Forest Beach and Conservation Lands, Chatham, 41.6700588 / -70.0253749; Chapin Beach, Dennis, 41.730314 / -70.2350271; Stauffer's Puddle, East Sandwich, 41.7620101 / -70.4762099

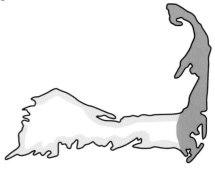

SEMIPALMATED SANDPIPER
Calidris pusilla

These tiny sandpipers travel in large flocks, often covering sections of beach during spring and fall migration.

Field marks: Breeding adult has gray-brown head, chest, back, and wings; short bill, white underside, black legs. Nonbreeding bird is similar but grayer.

Size: L: 6"–7", WS: 12"–14"

Similar species: Least sandpiper is smaller and has yellow-green legs and a slightly drooping bill. Western sandpiper is more rufous in breeding plumage, and its bill droops downward.

Season: Spring and fall migration

Habitat: Ocean and lake shorelines, tidal and freshwater mudflats

Food source: Insects, spiders, aquatic invertebrates, tiny shellfish

Nest: In a depression in the ground, in northern Canada and Alaska

Call: A measured *chirrup, chirrup*; a rattling, extended alarm call

Hot spots: Most beaches and mudflats bring in semi-palmated sandpipers during fall migration, so chances are you will find them wherever you go to look for more unusual shorebirds. These hot spots are proven favorites for larger flocks: Nauset Beach, Orleans, 41.7888489 / -69.9355316; Monomoy National Wildlife Refuge (and other nearby beaches), Chatham, 41.5913346 / -69.9880211; Long Pasture Wildlife Sanctuary, Barnstable, 41.70703 / -70.27171; Sandy Neck Beach, Barnstable, 41.7391369 / -70.3801775; Stauffer's Puddle, East Sandwich, 41.7620101 / -70.4762099

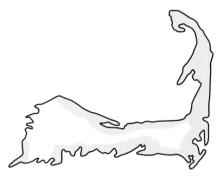

SHORT-BILLED DOWITCHER
Limnodromus griseus

Almost identical to the long-billed dowitcher, this one has spots on its breast and flanks instead of bars. Its call is strikingly different as well.

Field marks: Breeding adult has rufous head with white eye ring, black line through eye, long bill, orange breast and sides with black spots; scaly brown, black, and white pattern on wings and back; yellow legs. Nonbreeding bird is gray overall, with white eyebrow, white underside.

Size: L: 11"–12", WS: 19"–22"

Similar species: Long-billed dowitcher has a more musical call and bars instead of spots on its breast and flanks. Red knot is smaller and has a short bill.

Season: Spring and fall migration

Habitat: Marshes, mudflats, wetlands

Food source: Fly larvae and pupae, crab eggs, insects, some plants and seeds

Nest: On open tundra; southern Alaska

Call: A raspy *tcha-gri-gri, tcha-gri-gri*, spiraling down at the end

Hot spots: All the major shorebird hot spots on Cape Cod see flocks of short-billed dowitchers move through in spring and fall. The following spots can be dependable for the largest flocks: Lieutenant Island and Causeway, Wellfleet, 41.8960801 / -70.0161266; Coast Guard Beach, Eastham, 41.8344618 / -69.9453163; Monomoy National Wildlife Refuge, Chatham, 41.5913346 / -69.9880211; Nauset Marsh, Eastham, 41.8143142 / -69.9504232; Buck's Creek Marsh, Chatham, 41.673952 / -70.0011545

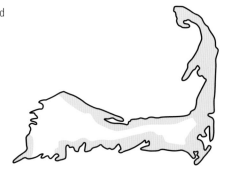

GREATER YELLOWLEGS
Tringa melanoleuca
Near-constant foraging behavior can make it tough to tell the two yellowlegs species apart (see photo inset for size comparison). Look for dark barring on the flanks and underside to pick out the greater yellowlegs.

Field marks: Black, gray, and white mottling overall; black streaks on head and neck, slightly upturned bill, white underside with black barring, yellow legs, white rump. In nonbreeding plumage, back and wings are browner.

Size: L: 14", WS: 23"–28"

Similar species: Lesser yellowlegs is shorter, has a straight bill, and has whiter flanks with no barring.

Season: Spring and fall migration

Habitat: Mudflats in salt- and freshwater marshes, open fields, pools, lakeshores

Food source: Small invertebrates, fish, frogs, seeds

Nest: In the open on a mudflat, in northern Canada

Call: Lyrical, continuous *pew-yoo, pew-yoo, pew-yoo*; also a three-note *tew-tew-tew* in flight

Hot spots: Lieutenant Island and Causeway, Wellfleet, 41.8960801 / -70.0161266; Coast Guard Beach, Eastham, 41.8344618 / -69.9453163; Bell's Neck Conservation Area, West Harwich, 41.6840342 / -70.1129007; Bass Creek, Dennis/Yarmouth Port, 41.723636 / -70.2378863; Stauffer's Puddle, East Sandwich, 41.7620101 / -70.4762099

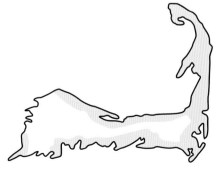

LESSER YELLOWLEGS
Tringa flavipes

The lesser yellowlegs' straight bill, clear underside, and shorter stature set it apart from its greater counterpart.

Field marks: Gray and white–streaked head and neck; mottled black and white breast, back, and wings; white underside, white rump, yellow legs. Mottling and streaking is muted in nonbreeding plumage.

Size: L: 10"–11", WS: 20"–24"

Similar species: Greater yellowlegs is up to 4 inches taller, has an upturned bill, and is barred with black on its underside in breeding season.

Season: Fall migration

Habitat: Fresh- and saltwater marshes, mudflats, open fields

Food source: Insects, invertebrates, seeds, tiny fish

Nest: On a pile of vegetation near water; northern Canada and west to Alaska

Call: *Tu-du* song singly and in pairs; also high-pitched, continuous notes as an alarm

Hot spots: Race Point Beach, Provincetown, 42.0691855 / -70.2381706; Lieutenant Island and Causeway, Wellfleet, 41.8960801 / -70.0161266; Monomoy National Wildlife Refuge, Chatham, 41.6568485 / -69.9582152; Forest Beach and Conservation Lands, Chatham, 41.6700588 / -70.0253749; Bell's Neck Conservation Area, West Harwich, 41.6840342 / -70.1129007

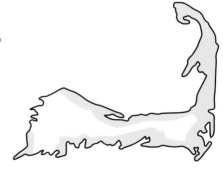

WILLET

Tringa semipalmata

The willet's white wing stripe makes it easy to spot as it arrives and lands on a beach or mudflat.

Field marks: Gray head, nape, wings, and back; long, straight gray bill with black tip; buffy breast with darker brown mottling, white underside with brownish barring, gray legs; wide white stripe on wings visible in flight. Nonbreeding adult is grayer overall with no barring.

Size: L: 15"–16", WS: 25"–30"

Similar species: Greater yellowlegs is darker, smaller, and has yellow legs.

Season: Spring and fall migration; summer on ocean coast

Habitat: Ocean coast—beaches and lagoons, tidal mudflats

Food source: Small crustaceans, insects, invertebrates, tiny fish

Nest: On a clump of grass or on open ground

Call: A continuous *willa-will-willa, willa-will-willa*

Hot spots: First Landing Park, Provincetown, 42.0368471 / -70.1967144; Great Island, Wellfleet, 41.9183734 / -70.0663376; Lieutenant Island and Causeway, Wellfleet, 41.8960801 / -70.0161266; Coast Guard Beach, Eastham, 41.8344618 / -69.9453163; Monomoy National Wildlife Refuge, Chatham, 41.6568485 / -69.9582152

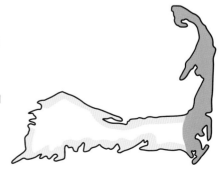

TURKEY

WILD TURKEY
Meleagris gallopavo
The nation's largest ground bird usually appears in flocks in grassy meadows.

Field marks: Large, heavy, iridescent body and thin, fleshy neck; rufous tail, orange legs. Male acquires long red wattles and a bright blue face and neck during breeding season, when he is often seen with his tail spread out in a fan shape.

Size: L: 44"–46", WS: 60"–64" (female much smaller: L: 37", WS: 50")

Similar species: Ring-necked pheasant is smaller, slimmer, and a lighter brown. Turkey vulture is smaller, has an all-red head and a much shorter tail.

Season: Year-round

Habitat: Oak and pine forests adjacent to open grassland

Food source: Plants, nuts, seeds, fruit, small invertebrates

Nest: On the ground at the base of a tree or hidden in masses of tall grasses and weeds

Call: A comical *gobble-gobble-gobble*, like a chuckle. Females have a *cluck-cluck* alarm call.

Hot spots: Farm fields, suburban backyards, roadsides from the rural hills to the interstate, and even city neighborhoods now have their own wild turkeys, so no hot spot is required to see them. The spectacular success of the turkey's reintroduction in the late 1960s and early 1970s is in evidence all around us—and some would say that it has long since gotten out of hand. If you'd like to see some, take a drive down a country road or hike along the edge of a woodland.

RAPTORS

TURKEY VULTURE
Cathartes aura
Soaring in kettles over virtually any landscape, this very large bird is easily recognized by its flight pattern.

Field marks: Large, black body; red featherless head, gray flight feathers for the entire length of each wing, rectangular tail. This vulture glides with wings held in a distinctive dihedral V.

Size: L: 26"–30", WS: 67"–72"

Similar species: Black vulture has gray head, black wings with gray-white "fingers" at the outer ends. Immature bald eagle has black-feathered head and all-black or mottled wings, which it holds flat.

Season: Spring through fall

Habitat: Soaring over open areas, including farmland, forests, ravines and gorges, ocean dunes, and plains

Food source: Carrion

Nest: In a crevice or dead tree

Call: Usually silent

Hot spots: Turkey vultures soar over open lands, highways, and populated areas in every part of Cape Cod from early spring to mid-fall, often in kettles of thirty or more birds. You should have no trouble seeing them gliding over US 6 as they search for the roadkill that drivers graciously provide for their daily repast.

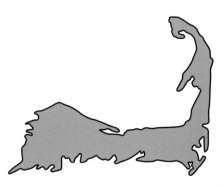

49

RED-TAILED HAWK
Buteo jamaicensis

The region's most common hawk is often seen near roadways, soaring over fields, or sitting at the tops of trees.

Field marks: Brown head and body with bright reddish-orange tail, usually visible in flight or at rest; white underside with brown streaks around the middle, forming a distinctive bellyband. Juvenile may be paler underneath and lack the red tail.

Size: L: 19"–25", WS: 46"–55"

Similar species: Broad-winged hawk is much smaller and has a black and white tail. Red-shouldered hawk has orange-banded chest, black tail with white stripes.

Season: Year-round

Habitat: Open fields, meadows, and marshes that have tall trees or other high perches; often seen in trees along major roadways

Food source: Primarily small mammals, but with a preference for red-winged blackbirds

Nest: In large trees

Call: A loud, hoarse *kee-e-e-r-r-rh*, the quintessential hawk call used in countless movies and television shows (and often attributed to the bald eagle)

Hot spots: Red-tailed hawks are the most common and widespread hawks on Cape Cod. You will see them standing atop utility poles and lampposts along highways, watching open areas from perches at the tops of trees, and being mobbed by starlings or crows when the hawk ventures too close to a nest. Look for the white chest and underside with a jagged gray-to-brown bellyband, as well as the bright rufous tail.

OSPREY
Pandion haliaetus
This fish-eating raptor is easily spotted near any major waterway.

Field marks: White head and face with black band from eye to shoulder, dark body and tail, white underside with streaky black breastband. Juvenile has buff-colored upper breast.

Size: L: 21"–24", WS: 56"–72"

Similar species: Bald eagle, often seen in the same habitat, is larger and has an all-white head and white tail.

Season: Summer

Habitat: Areas with open water that supports a healthy fish population; high perches

Food source: Fish

Nest: At the top of a tree or on a platform or crosspiece at the top of a utility pole or lamppost

Call: Very high *pip-pip-pip-pip*

Hot spots: Go to the seashore or the nearest river or marsh. Look for a large nest made of twigs at the top of a utility pole or other high platform. Check this out with binoculars to see if there's an osprey sitting in the nest; if not, chances are good there's one within a few hundred yards. These very common "fish hawks" are never far from water and very attentive to their nests.

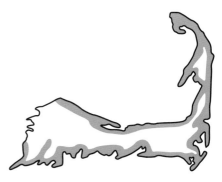

DOVE AND PIGEON

MOURNING DOVE
Zenaida macroura

A resident of suburban yards, parks, and shopping centers, this gentle creature can be seen and heard virtually anywhere in New England.

Field marks: Light grayish brown overall with a black spot on the cheek and black spots on the wings; short, thin bill; long tail expands in flight to show white tips with a black edge; whitish undertail coverts.

Size: L: 12", WS: 17"–19"

Similar species: Rock pigeon is larger and heavier, and is either light gray and black or a combination of colors due to interbreeding with other dove species. There are no other doves regularly found on Cape Cod.

Season: Year-round

Habitat: Mowed lawns and platform or ground feeders in residential areas, parks with trees and shrubs, and other areas frequented by people

Food source: Seeds, leaves, and plant matter found on the ground

Nest: In a tree, shrub, or on the ground

Call: A slow, mournful *ohh-WOO, hoo, hoo*; also a pronounced whistling made by the wings during flight

Hot spots: Mourning doves are found throughout residential areas and are easy to locate. They readily come to platform and ground feeders in backyards, and usually become daily visitors. Watch utility wires in your area for single birds, pairs, and flocks.

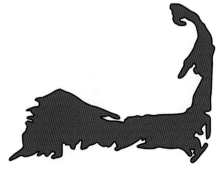

ROCK PIGEON
Columba livia

An introduced species from Europe, this member of the dove family (formerly known as rock dove or feral pigeon) took full advantage of its new territory and is now found on every city street in the country.

Field marks: Original coloring is a purple head, iridescent blue neck and breast, light gray back and upper wings, darker gray primary flight feathers, black stripe across both wings, black trailing edge; white rump, gray tail with a black tip. Interbreeding with domestic species has produced a variety of alternate plumages in mottled shades of brown, black, gray, and white.

Size: L: 12.5"–14", WS: 26"–34"

Similar species: Mourning dove is smaller, more delicate, and is always grayish-brown with black spots on wings.

Season: Year-round

Habitat: Areas inhabited by humans, including cities, suburbs, buildings and barnyards in rural areas, also on agricultural lands

Food source: Seeds, berries, and human discards scavenged from streets, yards, and parks

Nest: On man-made ledges—windowsills, bridge girders, eaves, gutters, etc.

Call: Elongated, descending *coo* with a throaty rumble

Hot spots: Rock pigeons are everywhere humans are. Check streets, gravel driveways, parking lots, rooftops of houses and barns, landfills, dumpsters, restaurants with outdoor dining, fairs and festivals, and other places where people may drop a morsel of food.

HUMMINGBIRD

RUBY-THROATED HUMMINGBIRD
Archilochus colubris

The eastern United States has only one reliable resident hummingbird, this sparkling jewel that readily comes to backyard feeders.

Field marks: Male has green cap and back, black bar through eye under cap, bright red throat, white breast, green sides, gray wings, gray and black tail with white wing tips. Female lacks the red throat.

Size: L: 3"–3.75", WS: 4.5"

Similar species: Rufous hummingbird (accidental in New England) has a bright orange throat and underside, orange at the base of the tail.

Season: Spring migration; summer

Habitat: Backyards, parks, other areas with nectar-producing flowers; open woodlands

Food source: Nectar from red and orange flowers; some insects

Nest: Fastened to a tree branch with spiderweb silk

Call: Tiny, squeaky chip note repeated in rapid succession, sometimes in quick triplets

Hot spots: If you don't have a backyard with a hummingbird feeder, these spots are productive because of the trumpet vine, honeysuckle, cardinal flower, and other appropriate blooms that grow in them: Wellfleet Bay Wildlife Sanctuary, Wellfleet, 41.8825315 / -69.995712; Fort Hill, Eastham, 41.818792 / -69.9644995; Monomoy National Wildlife Refuge, Morris Island, Chatham, 41.6568485 / -69.9582152; Bell's Neck Conservation Area, West Harwich, 41.6840342 / -70.1129007; Long Pasture Wildlife Sanctuary, Barnstable, 41.70703 / -70.27171

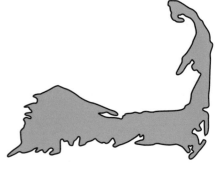

KINGFISHER

BELTED KINGFISHER
Megaceryle alcyon

Hunting over moving streams, rivers, ponds, and lakes, the easily recognized kingfisher can be fascinating to watch.

Field marks: Male has blue crest and face to just below the long bill, white collar, blue breast band over white breast, blue wings and back, white underside, blue tail with white bands. Female has a rust-colored band below the blue breastband and some rust on flanks under the wings.

Size: L: 12"–14", WS: 20"–24"

Similar species: Pileated woodpecker is larger and has a bright red crest (and is not found on Cape Cod).

Season: Year-round

Habitat: Ponds, lakes, rivers, streams, saltwater waterways

Food source: Fish, mollusks, crustaceans, small reptiles, amphibians, small mammals

Nest: The adults dig a tunnel in a riverbank and lay the eggs at the far end.

Call: Long, loud rattling *ak-ak-ak-ak-ak*, often in flight

Hot spots: Just about every pond on Cape Cod has a resident kingfisher. Before you drive to one of these hot spots, check the ponds and rivers near your location. Pilgrim Lake, North Truro, 42.05796 / -70.1277924; Wellfleet Bay Wildlife Sanctuary, Wellfleet, 41.8825315 / -69.995712; Town Cove, Orleans, 41.787633 / -69.9854636; Mill Pond, Marstons Mills, 41.6515912 / -70.4144454; Old Fish Hatchery and Nye Pond, East Sandwich, 41.7286493 / -70.4315861

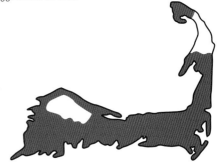

WOODPECKERS

RED-BELLIED WOODPECKER

Melanerpes carolinus

A year-round resident, this midsize woodpecker with a bright red cap readily comes to suet and peanut feeders.

Field marks: Male has red cap extending from bill to shoulder; buff face, breast, and underside; black and white barred back and wings, black trailing edge and wing primaries, white rump, black and white tail. Female's cap begins at the top of the head, leaving a buff forehead.

Size: L: 9"–10", WS: 16"–18"

Similar species: Yellow-bellied sapsucker has red cap, but its nape is white and it has a distinctive black and white facial pattern. Northern flicker has brown back with black barring, considerable spotting on buff breast, black bib, and gray cap with small red spot.

Season: Year-round

Habitat: Open woodlands, parks, backyards

Food source: Insects, seeds, fruit, suet, tree sap

Nest: In a tree cavity excavated by the pair or used in previous years by other woodpeckers

Call: Simple, mid-pitched *quirr* is most familiar; also chattering *kik-kik-kik-kik-kik*.

Hot spots: Any wooded area on the Cape has at least one family of red-bellied woodpeckers, and a morning walk along a forest trail may reveal half a dozen individuals or more. Active and expressive, they make themselves known with considerable movement up tree trunks and with their easily recognizable calls. You are sure to come across them as you look for more uncommon birds in the woods.

DOWNY WOODPECKER
Dryobates pubescens
The smallest woodpecker in North America is also one of the most common, coming readily to feeders and nesting in neighborhoods with large trees.

Field marks: Male has black and white head with red spot on back of crown, small bill with white tuft at its base, black wings barred in white, large white patch on back, white breast and underside, dark tail. Female is identical but lacks the red spot.

Size: L: 6.75", WS: 11"–12"

Similar species: Hairy woodpecker is larger, and its bill is about twice the length.

Season: Year-round

Habitat: Deciduous forests, parks and backyards with leafy trees

Food source: Seeds, suet, nuts, insects

Nest: In a natural or excavated hole in a tree

Call: Elongated, descending *ti-ti-TI-ti-ti-ti-ti-ti*; alternate is a high-pitched, one-note *tik*.

Hot spots: Downy woodpeckers are very common and easily spotted in any area with a healthy stand of trees. Look for them in local parks, woodlands, or backyards with mature trees in your neighborhood, or attract them to your own backyard with a suet or peanut feeder.

HAIRY WOODPECKER
Dryobates villosus

Larger than a downy, with a longer bill, hairy woodpeckers are otherwise nearly identical to the smaller bird. Vocal cues can help determine which is which.

Field marks: Male has black and white head with red spot on back of crown, long bill, black wings barred in white, large white patch on back, white breast and underside, dark tail. Female is identical but lacks the red spot.

Size: L: 9"–10", WS: 15"–17"

Similar species: Downy woodpecker is smaller, has a white tuft at the base of the bill, and has a shorter bill.

Season: Year-round

Habitat: Deciduous forests, parks, and neighborhoods with stands of mature trees

Food source: Gypsy moth caterpillars, spiders, insects, berries, seeds, nuts, suet

Nest: In a natural or excavated hole in a tree

Call: A single *pik*, followed by a long, high-pitched rattle; also *weeka, weeka, weeka*, like a squeaky wheel

Hot spots: Common and widespread in neighborhoods, hairy woodpeckers will come repeatedly to suet and peanut feeders when natural foods are not available (winter and early spring). You also can find these birds in parks with woodlands, both in wilderness areas and in the heart of towns.

NORTHERN FLICKER
Colaptes auratus

Of the two races of northern flickers found across the country, the eastern variety is the yellow-shafted flicker. The yellow underwing offers proof of this.

Field marks: Male has gray head, light brown face, red spot on back of head, black malar stripe, black eye, long bill. Buff breast with many black spots, black bib at throat; back and wings are light brown and heavily barred with black; white rump is visible in flight. Tail is black with white barring. Female lacks red spot and black malar.

Size: L: 12"–14", WS: 19"–21"

Similar species: Yellow-bellied sapsucker has red throat and no brown areas.

Season: Spring and summer

Habitat: Open woodlands and edges, parks with mature trees, neighborhoods

Food source: Ants and other insects, fruit and berries, suet, nuts, sunflower seed from feeders

Nest: In a tree cavity or a hole in a utility pole; also in man-made birdhouses

Call: A rapid, repeated *flicker-flicker-flicker-flicker*, also a squeakier *wikka-wikka-wikka* call while interacting with other birds

Hot spots: Nearly every forest, park with mature trees, and neighborhood has a pair or colony of flickers within it. Flickers come to suet and nut feeders, especially platform feeders that allow them to stand horizontally and eat rather than perching or grabbing the mesh of a cage feeder. They are also seen frequently feeding on the ground after a rain, when ants are forced out of their nests.

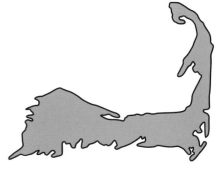

FLYCATCHERS

EASTERN WOOD-PEWEE
Contopus virens

This common summer resident breeds in hardwood forests. Listen for the call that gives the bird its name.

Field marks: Gray head with crest, thin eye ring, gray back, black wings with clearly visible white wing bars, grayish breast resembling a vest, yellowish underside, white undertail coverts, long dark tail.

Size: L: 6.25", WS: 10"

Similar species: Eastern phoebe is darker and stockier overall. Willow and alder flycatchers are smaller, with brighter wing bars and whiter underside.

Season: Summer

Habitat: Hardwood forests, parks, suburban neighborhoods with mature trees

Food source: Flying insects

Nest: Built on the end of a tree branch

Call: A single *peeeoowee,* or repeated *peee-wee*, rising at the end

Hot spots: Beech Forest, Provincetown, 42.0670802 / -70.1953679; Wellfleet Bay Wildlife Sanctuary, Wellfleet, 41.8825315 / -69.995712; Fort Hill, Eastham, 41.818792 / -69.9644995; Nickerson State Park, Brewster, 41.7540898 / -70.0206757; Bell's Neck Conservation Area, West Harwich, 41.6840342 / -70.1129007; Santuit Pond, Mashpee, 41.6552018 / -70.4597425

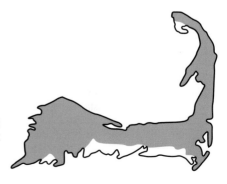

EASTERN PHOEBE
Sayornis phoebe

Like a flycatcher but larger, phoebes make themselves known with their tail-flicking behavior and distinctive song.

Field marks: Dark gray head, black bill, lighter gray nape and back, gray-smudged breast, pale yellowish underside, gray wings with no wing bars; long, straight tail.

Size: L: 7", WS: 10.5"–11.5"

Similar species: Eastern wood-pewee is smaller and lighter colored. All other local flycatchers have some kind of eye ring and wing bars.

Season: Summer

Habitat: Woodlands near open grasslands, pastures, or farms; suburban neighborhoods

Food source: Flying insects, berries, small fish caught from the water's surface

Nest: Glued with mud to the side of a building or in a tree on top of an old nest

Call: A high, hoarse *PHEE-bee*, or quieter *tu-oo*

Hot spots: Any walk in the woods during mating and breeding seasons will yield at least one phoebe sighting; a focused birding day may turn up several. Wellfleet Bay Wildlife Sanctuary, Wellfleet, 41.8825315 / -69.995712; Fort Hill, Eastham, 41.818792 / -69.9644995; Nickerson State Park, Brewster, 41.7540898 / -70.0206757; Cape Cod Organic Farm, Barnstable, 41.6979064 / -70.2887732; Frances A. Crane Wildlife Management Area, East Falmouth, 41.6348031 / -70.5607738

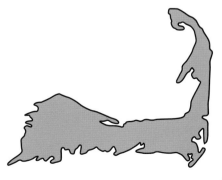

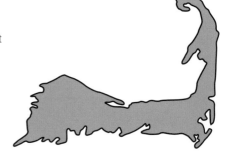

GREAT-CRESTED FLYCATCHER
Myiarchus crinitus

With its bright yellow underside and rusty orange tail, the largest local flycatcher provides plenty of hints to its identification.

Field marks: Gray-brown head with pronounced crest, paler throat, heavy black bill with pale pink base, olive back, dark wings with rufous primaries, white tips on flight feathers, gray breast, yellow underside, rufous tail.

Size: L: 8.5"–8.75", WS: 12"–14"

Similar species: Eastern phoebe is smaller and darker overall, with a dark gray tail.

Season: Summer

Habitat: Woodlands with hardwood trees

Food source: Flying and crawling insects, caterpillars, butterflies, berries

Nest: In a natural or woodpecker-excavated cavity of a tree or in a man-made bird box

Call: One-syllable *wheeep*, often several in succession; also raspy *brrp, brrp, brrp*, repeated continuously

Hot spots: Foss Woods, Provincetown, 42.0643802 / -70.1584125; Wellfleet Bay Wildlife Sanctuary, Wellfleet, 41.8825315 / -69.995712; Fort Hill, Eastham, 41.818792 / -69.9644995; Bell's Neck Conservation Area, West Harwich, 41.6840342 / -70.1129007; Santuit Pond, Mashpee, 41.6552018 / -70.4597425

EASTERN KINGBIRD
Tyrannus tyrannus

A black, gray, and white bird of open grasslands, the Northeast's only kingbird is easily identified by the white tip of its tail.

Field marks: Black head, gray back, white throat, grayish breast, white underside, dark gray wings, long black tail with white tip.

Size: L: 8.5", WS: 14"–15"

Similar species: Eastern phoebe is smaller, darker, has a yellowish wash on its underparts, and has no white tip on its tail.

Season: Summer

Habitat: Open grasslands, meadows, and farmland, where it often perches on fences and posts.

Food source: Insects, berries, fruit

Nest: On a tree branch or inside a barn or other structure

Call: Very high-pitched *dit-dit-dit-dit-dit-dit-derWEE, derWEE*; also a single *chee* note

Hot spots: Any open area bordered by a fence may attract kingbirds. These spots see multiple birds throughout the spring and summer: Beech Forest, Provincetown, 42.0670802 / -70.1953679; High Head, Pilgrim Heights, Provincetown, 42.0563031 / -70.1161194; Fort Hill, Eastham, 41.818792 / -69.9644995; Bell's Neck Conservation Area, West Harwich, 41.6840342 / -70.1129007; Long Pasture Wildlife Sanctuary, Barnstable, 41.70703 / -70.27171

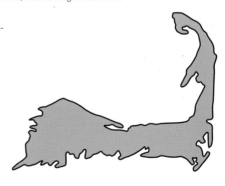

JAY

BLUE JAY
Cyanocitta cristata

Brightly colored, loud, and aggressive, the blue jay dominates bird feeders, neighborhoods, wooded parks, and forests throughout the eastern United States.

Field marks: Blue crest, black and white face, black bill, black ring across chest, white throat and underside, grayish breast, blue back and wings with one bright white wing bar, white tips on secondary flight feathers, long blue tail with white outer tips.

Size: L: 11", WS: 16"

Similar species: Canada jay has no blue features. Eastern bluebird is smaller and has an all-blue mantle and ruddy breast.

Season: Year-round

Habitat: Wooded areas in neighborhoods and parks, forest edges, backyards

Food source: Seeds, nuts, fruit, berries, insects, very small rodents and reptiles, eggs from birds' nests

Nest: In trees, often close to the trunk; most likely in conifers

Call: A harsh *jaaaay*, singly or repeated four or five times; also mimic calls (mewing catbird, red-tailed hawk, and others), and a descending warble often compared to a rusty hinge

Hot spots: A popular and often numerous backyard bird, blue jays can be found in any yard with a feeder stocked with sunflower seeds or peanut pick-outs, as well as in neighborhood parks or random stands of mature trees.

CROW

AMERICAN CROW
Corvus brachyrhynchos
Easily spotted in neighborhoods and parking lots, on buildings and beaches, and in large flocks in parks and wooded areas, crows are among the most common birds in America.

Field marks: All black with a long, solid black bill; wide wings, a short tail that fans in flight. Crows flap their wings continuously in flight.

Size: L: 17.5", WS: 35"–40"

Similar species: Common raven soars and glides in flight and has scruffy throat feathers and a wedge-shaped tail. Fish crow is virtually identical but has a higher, nasal call.

Season: Year-round

Habitat: Open fields, woods, ocean coastline, beaches, areas inhabited by humans

Food source: Carrion, scraps scavenged from human discards, fruit, seeds, small animals and birds, bird eggs, insects

Nest: High in a tree, often more than 90 feet up

Call: The familiar *caw, caw*, also a rhythmic *caw-haw, cah-caw-haw* and a staccato series of clicks

Hot spots: Look in any parking area, on any beach, or in parks with mowed lawns to find this ubiquitous bird, as well as in your own backyard if you feed birds with a platform or ground feeder.

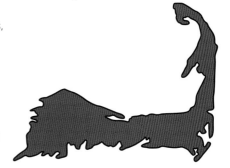

SWALLOWS

PURPLE MARTIN
Progne subis

This colony nester often lives in man-made houses built for martins, near a water feature or ocean beach.

Field marks: Male is deep purple-blue overall, with a small black bill and wings as long as its slightly forked tail. Female has deep blue cap, back, wings, and tail; gray forehead and collar, gray-smudged breast.

Size: L: 7.5"–8.5", WS: 16"–18"

Similar species: All swallow species are smaller. Tree swallow has bright white underparts. Cliff swallow has an orange face and grayish underparts with a rufous wash.

Season: Summer

Habitat: Woodlands, neighborhoods, and open fields near a prominent water feature (ocean, bay, lake, river)

Food source: Flying insects

Nest: In colonies in a man-made martin house or in a series of tree cavities in a woodland area

Call: A series of chirps, whistles, and gurgles on many pitches, differing between male and female birds; also a simple *seet, sset seet*

Hot spots: Many coastal neighborhoods have martin houses that can be viewed easily from residential streets, but these are private property, so I can't list them here. The following public areas also host martin colonies throughout spring and summer: Wellfleet Bay Wildlife Sanctuary, Wellfleet, 41.8825315 / -69.995712; Long Pasture Wildlife Sanctuary, Barnstable, 41.70703 / -70.27171; South Cape Beach State Park, Mashpee, 41.5536361 / -70.4993146; Santuit Pond, Mashpee, 41.6552018 / -70.4597425; Frances A. Crane Wildlife Management Area, East Falmouth, 41.6348031 / -70.5607738

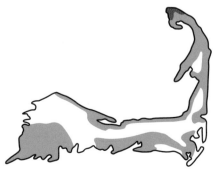

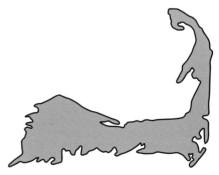

TREE SWALLOW
Tachycineta bicolor
The bright blue tree swallow often nests in boxes meant for eastern bluebirds.

Field marks: Male has bright blue head, back, and rump with white undertail coverts; bright white throat, breast, and underside; black wings and tail; tail is slightly forked. Female is gray above and white below.

Size: L: 5.75", WS: 12.5"–14.5"

Similar species: Cliff swallow has a rufous face, dark throat, and a grayish white breast with rufous streaks. Barn swallow has a darker blue back, an orange face and lighter orange underside, and a deeply forked tail.

Season: Spring and summer

Habitat: Open fields with stands of trees near marshes, swamps, lakeshores, rivers, or ponds

Food source: Flying and crawling insects, spiders

Nest: In boxes usually meant for bluebirds; also in tree cavities

Call: High-pitched, buzzy, chattery *cheet-cheet-cheet* calls with variations in speed and pitch; also simple *treet* note in flight

Hot spots: When you visit any salt marsh, riverside, lakeshore, or other body of water in spring and summer, tree swallows will be very much in evidence. Darting back and forth over the water to catch mosquitoes and other flying insects, they rarely stop to allow you a long look, but you will have the chance to admire their bright blue backs and wings as they glide by you. Tree swallows are abundant on Cape Cod, and they make their processes of feeding and breeding remarkably easy to view.

BARN SWALLOW
Hirundo rustica

The bird that gives all swallowtails their name, this brightly colored summer resident nests in barns, garages, carports, and other structures with open eaves.

Field marks: Male has dark blue cap, mask, back, wings, and tail; orange face and throat, lighter orange breast and underside; long, deeply forked tail. Female has a somewhat whiter underside.

Size: L: 6.75"–7.5", WS: 13"–15"

Similar species: Cliff swallow has a gray collar and underside, a duller orange face, and a dark blue throat.

Season: Spring and summer

Habitat: Open fields with barns, neighborhoods, lakes, wetlands

Food source: Insects of open fields: grasshoppers, crickets, moths, and others

Nest: In colonies, in the corners of barns and garages or under bridges

Call: High-pitched, constant chatter in groups of three or four notes; also a *chee-deep* chip note

Hot spots: Barn swallows can be found in any area of open land, especially if there is a structure—a bridge, pavilion, barn, or porch—under which they can build nests. A summer drive through agricultural lands or through your favorite wildlife management area will almost certainly yield views of barn swallows hunting down insects. Watch the utility wires along these roadsides for rows of swallows (which may include tree swallows and purple martins).

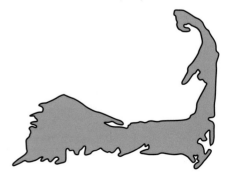

TITMOUSE AND CHICKADEE

TUFTED TITMOUSE
Baeolophus bicolor
From forests to feeders, this friend of black-capped chickadees is a dependable sighting on any woodland outing.

Field marks: Gray crest, back of head, back, wings, and tail; white face with large black eye and black forehead; grayish-white throat, breast, and underside; light orange flanks, white undertail coverts.

Size: L: 6.5", WS: 9.75"–10.75"

Similar species: Blue-gray gnatcatcher is smaller, has no crest, and has a white eye ring and a black tail. Warbling vireo has no crest or orange flanks.

Season: Year-round

Habitat: Deciduous forests, neighborhoods with mature trees, parks, backyards

Food source: Insects, spiders, nuts, seeds, suet

Nest: In a tree cavity or birdhouse

Call: A musical *peter, peter, peter, peter*; also a rough, scolding *shrii, shrii, shrii* and a series of very high *ti, ti, ti* sounds

Hot spots: Tufted titmouse is one of the most common birds of the Cape Cod woodlands and neighborhoods, and virtually every backyard feeder filled with sunflower seeds receives daily visits from this bird. The titmouse often associates with black-capped chickadees, so if you're on a woodland walk and you haven't detected a titmouse, watch groups of chickadees to see which of their many allies they have with them.

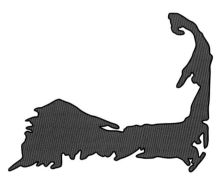

69

BLACK-CAPPED CHICKADEE
Poecile atricapillus
Cheeky, curious, and the first to scold you when your feeder runs out of seed, this chickadee is an indispensable resident of any backyard habitat or wooded area.

Field marks: Black cap and throat, white face and nape, gray back, black wings, white edges on secondaries, white breast, buff flanks, dark gray tail.

Size: L: 5.25"–5.5", WS: 7.5"–8.5"

Similar species: Boreal chickadee has a brown cap and pinkish-brown flanks.

Season: Year-round

Habitat: Deciduous and mixed woods, neighborhoods with mature trees, parks, backyards

Food source: Seeds, berries, insects, suet

Nest: In a tree cavity or nest box, sometimes at human eye level but usually as much as 40 feet up

Call: The familiar *chicka-dee-dee-dee*; also a long whistled *yoo-hoo*

Hot spots: It's easy to spot black-capped chickadees at feeders, on the edges of park woodlands, and on just about any trail through woods or forest. In some parks, chickadees have been conditioned to approach people on nature trails to beg for sunflower seeds. If the park you're in permits this and you wish to participate, carry a small bag of sunflower seeds or broken-up peanuts and wait for the birds to come to you. The chickadees are not shy; you will know if they are accustomed to hand-feeding.

NUTHATCHES

RED-BREASTED NUTHATCH
Sitta canadensis
The smaller of the two Cape Cod nuthatches makes the region its year-round residence.

Field marks: Male has black cap and eye stripe, white eyebrow and throat, sharp black bill, red-orange underparts, gray-blue back and tail, white stripes on outer tail feathers. Female is slightly less brightly colored.

Size: L: 4.5", WS: 8"–8.5"

Similar species: White-breasted nuthatch is larger, lacks the eye stripe, and has a white breast.

Season: Year-round

Habitat: Coniferous forests, as well as backyards and feeders in northern neighborhoods with many conifers

Food source: Nuts, seeds, insects, spiders, clusters of insect eggs

Nest: In a tree cavity

Call: *Toot, toot, toot*, like a toy horn; also an extended trill

Hot spots: In thickly forested areas of Cape Cod, red-breasted nuthatches can be found at virtually every trailhead, and many will pester you for sunflower seeds. It's not uncommon to have one of these birds dive-bomb your head or land on your shoulder in hopes that you will produce a handful of seeds. Even if a nuthatch does not approach you directly, their toy-horn tooting is a familiar sound in forests. They also come readily to backyard suet and sunflower seed feeders.

WHITE-BREASTED NUTHATCH
Sitta carolinensis

Feeding upside down on a tree trunk, the larger local nuthatch frequents feeders as well as mature trees.

Field marks: Black cap, white face, black eye; long, upturned bill; gray back and wings, white breast and underparts, rufous tinted undertail coverts (white in female), gray tail.

Size: L: 5"–6", WS: 10"–11"

Similar species: Red-breasted nuthatch is smaller, has a black eye stripe, and has reddish underparts.

Season: Year-round

Habitat: Mixed forests with oak trees, neighborhoods with mature trees, parks

Food source: Insects, seeds, nuts, suet

Nest: In a nest box, tree cavity, or hole abandoned by woodpeckers

Call: A honking *waah, waah, waah, waah*, all on one note; also a faster series of a single higher note

Hot spots: White-breasted nuthatch is one of the most entertaining of the common feeder birds, hanging upside down on suet or peanut feeders and pecking away for several minutes at a time, or sitting on platform feeders and shooing the house sparrows away. It's also very much in evidence in suburban woodlands and city parks. Nuthatches usually announce themselves before flying in to take a closer look at you from the comfort of a nearby tree trunk.

WRENS

CAROLINA WREN
Thryothorus ludovicianus

Don't be deceived by the name—this expressive wren's range has expanded northward, with Cape Cod as a top destination.

Field marks: Brown cap, bright white eyebrow edged in black, brown eye line, buff cheek, white throat; buff-orange chest, flanks, and underside; brown back, brown wings barred in black, white undertail coverts with black barring, short brown tail.

Size: L: 5.5", WS: 7.5"

Similar species: All other local wrens are smaller. Marsh wren has white eyebrow, but its crown is black.

Season: Year-round

Habitat: Edges of woodlands with lots of brushy shrubs

Food source: Insects, spiders

Nest: In a crack between rocks or in a crevice or hole in a building

Call: Often transcribed as *teakettle, teakettle, teakettle*; sometimes very quick, but often slower

Hot spots: Carolina wrens are widespread and numerous in New England, and they should be fairly easy to find because of their enthusiastic and highly recognizable song. Here are some places where birders regularly report multiple Carolina wrens: Herring River, Wellfleet, 41.9348807 / -70.0597715; Cape Cod National Seashore, Salt Pond Visitor Center, Eastham, 41.837154 / -69.9726588; Brewster Community Gardens, Brewster, 41.7608126 / -70.0901663; Cape Cod Organic Farm, Barnstable, 41.6979064 / -70.2887732; Santuit Pond, Mashpee, 41.6552018 / -70.4597425

HOUSE WREN
Troglodytes aedon

Tiny birds with a lot to say, house wrens often nest in man-made boxes in residential areas.

Field marks: Light brown (or light gray) head and body with buff or pale gray throat and breast; faint white eyebrow and long, downward-curving yellow bill; brownish (or grayish) wings with darker horizontal barring. Both brown and gray individuals have warm brown undertail coverts and tail with black barring; tail is often held upright at a nearly 90-degree angle from the body.

Size: L: 4"–5", WS: 6"–7"

Similar species: Winter wren is smaller and more distinctly barred. Carolina wren is larger, more rufous, and has a bright white eyebrow extending from bill to nape. Sedge wren and marsh wren are generally not seen in the same habitat as house wren.

Season: Spring and fall migration and throughout the summer

Habitat: Wooded areas in parks, neighborhoods, and along farm fields, as well as in forest thickets and shrubs

Food source: Insects found on trees and shrubs, caterpillars, spiders

Nest: In a sheltered opening in a shrub, a tree cavity, or a man-made nest box

Call: One of the most exuberant in the avian kingdom: a series of musical trills, whistles, and phrases sung without breaks and repeated note for note at regular intervals

Hot spots: As the "house" in its name suggests, house wrens are comfortable sharing neighborhoods with human beings. If you don't have one in your residential area, here are some spots where birders have seen them regularly, and often in quantity: Wellfleet Bay Wildlife Sanctuary, Wellfleet, 41.8825315 / -69.995712; Fort Hill, Eastham, 41.818792 / -69.9644995; Long Pasture Wildlife Sanctuary, Barnstable, 41.70703 / -70.27171; Ashumet Holly Wildlife Sanctuary (Mass Audubon), Falmouth, 41.62315 / -70.53616; Santuit Pond, Mashpee, 41.6552018 / -70.4597425

BLUE-GRAY GNATCATCHER
Polioptila caerulea

The unbroken color, bright white eye ring, and long, black tail with white outer feathers will help you identify this frenetic bird.

Field marks: Bright blue-gray cap, nape, and back; black forehead (male only), gray cheek, whitish throat, grayish-white breast and underside, gray wings with white tertials, black tail with white outer feathers.

Size: L: 4.25"–4.5", WS: 6"–6.75"

Similar species: Warbling vireo has no cap or eye ring, has a pale white eyebrow, and is plain gray above and whitish below with yellowish flanks.

Season: Spring and fall migration

Habitat: Deciduous woodlands

Food source: Gnats, as well as many other insects, butterflies, spiders, bees, and wasps

Nest: Fastened to a tree branch, with no specific height preference

Call: *Bees, bu-bu-bees, bees,* with a buzzy spiraling downward note on each *bees*; also a *speez, speez, speez* call, all on one note

Hot spots: Clapps Pond, Provincetown, 42.0532441 / -70.2098465; Monomoy National Wildlife Refuge, Chatham, 41.6568485 / -69.9582152; Bell's Neck Conservation Area, West Harwich, 41.6840342 / -70.1129007; Santuit Pond, Mashpee, 41.6552018 / -70.4597425; Falmouth Town Forest, Falmouth, 41.5755171 / -70.6132507

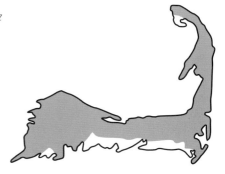

THRUSHES

EASTERN BLUEBIRD
Sialia sialis

Bright blue above and bright orange below, this folk symbol of happiness battles all spring and summer to keep its nest box, eggs, and nestlings safe from house sparrows and other aggressive raiders.

Field marks: Male has bright blue head, back, wings, and tail; orange throat, breast, and flanks; white belly and undertail coverts, black primaries. Female has gray head and back, blue leading edge of wing and primaries; light orange throat, breast, and flanks; white belly and undertail, blue tail.

Size: L: 7"–7.75", WS: 12"–13"

Similar species: Cerulean warbler is smaller, has black streaks on its flanks and two white wing bars, and lacks the orange throat and breast. Black-throated blue warbler is smaller and has a black face, black stripe on flanks, and no orange. Blue jay is much larger, has a high crest and a white breast, and has no orange.

Season: Winter north of Wellfleet; year-round throughout Upper Cape

Habitat: Open grasslands, parks with grassy areas and trees, scrubby areas along beaches

Food source: Insects and invertebrates; readily comes to mealworm feeders in backyards

Nest: In a tree cavity, nest box, disused woodpecker hole, or a hole in a utility pole

Call: A short series of syrupy notes and trills, sometimes interlaced with sharp, raspy *chic* notes

Hot spots: Marconi Station Site, Wellfleet, 41.9140224 / -69.9714196; Wellfleet Bay Wildlife Sanctuary, Wellfleet, 41.8825315 / -69.995712; Harwich Community Garden, Harwich, 41.6746909 / -70.0910568; Crowes Pasture, Dennis, 41.7566589 / -70.1302707; Bell's Neck Conservation Area, West Harwich, 41.6840342 / -70.1129007

AMERICAN ROBIN
Turdus migratorius

The unofficial harbinger of spring, robins grace every mowed lawn, park, neighborhood, wooded area, and roadside rest stop in North America.

Field marks: Dark gray head, broken white eye ring, yellow bill, thin white lines on throat, bright orange breast and belly, white undertail coverts, gray back and wings, gray tail with white outermost tail feathers. Juveniles have a lighter breast and belly covered in gray spots.

Size: L: 10", WS: 14"–17"

Similar species: Eastern towhee has an all-black head, white breast, and rufous flanks. Female eastern bluebird is smaller, a lighter gray overall, and has blue wing feathers.

Season: Year-round

Habitat: Open woodlands, neighborhoods, commercial and industrial areas with mowed lawns, gardens, farm fields, and grasslands with trees

Food source: Worms, grubs, berries, fruit, some insects

Nest: In a tree or on a man-made platform under shelter (like the joist of a porch roof), often in full view

Call: Series of musical notes and triplets with brief pauses: *wheedie, wee, wheedio, wheedie, wee*; also a less-melodious five-note phrase: *chi-chi-chi-chi-chi*

Hot spots: Look out any window onto a lawn in spring and summer, and robins will be performing their hop-and-listen behavior as they hunt for invertebrates just under the ground's surface. Every neighborhood and commercial district becomes a robin hot spot once the late winter snow begins to thaw and bare ground appears.

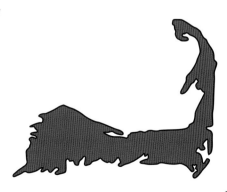

GRAY CATBIRD
Dumetella carolinensis

The catbird's trademark *mew* call is not the only unique thing about it. It's also the only solidly bill-to-tail gray bird in North America.

Field marks: Uniformly gray with a black cap, black eye, rufous undertail coverts, and black tail.

Size: L: 8.5"–9", WS: 11"–12"

Similar species: Northern mockingbird is gray above and whitish below, with large white patches on its wings.

Season: Summer

Habitat: Forest and marsh edges, wooded edges of farm fields and grasslands, neighborhoods with mature trees

Food source: Insects, spiders, fruit, seeds; sometimes comes to jelly feeders used by orioles

Nest: In the lower branches of a tree or in a shrub

Call: A chattery series of notes that may vary from one bird to the next, derived from the catbird's ability to mimic other birds; also a single *mew* note, very like a cat

Hot spots: Every city park, neighborhood, cemetery, nature center, sanctuary, forest, and farm has its resident catbird, and many of these areas have several. The only places you are not likely to encounter these birds is in areas of dense forests with few discernible edges.

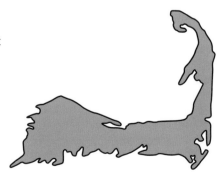

NORTHERN MOCKINGBIRD
Mimus polyglottos

Nicely adapted to city parks, neighborhoods, cemeteries, and other human-inhabited areas, the mockingbird can incorporate everything from other birds' calls to car alarms in its own song.

Field marks: Gray cap, nape, and back; black eye line, yellow eye, white lores; white throat, breast, and belly; darker wings with two wing bars, large white wing patches, visible during flight; white undertail coverts; long, dark tail often held at an upward angle.

Size: L: 9"–10", WS: 12"–14"

Similar species: Gray catbird is uniformly gray all over. Northern shrike has a black mask, black wings, and a black tail. American pipit is smaller, has a light breast with black streaks, and is found on open ground like beaches and fallow fields.

Season: Year-round

Habitat: Parks, neighborhoods, farmland with hedgerows and wooded areas

Food source: Many kinds of insects, fruit, worms, some small reptiles

Nest: In shrubs or low in trees

Call: Varied phrases that may be different from one bird to the next. Each mimicked call is usually repeated in sets of five or six, and may incorporate the songs of killdeer, Carolina wren, Baltimore oriole, ovenbird, and a wide range of others. Some have learned to imitate car alarms, emergency vehicle sirens, and the beeping of construction vehicles backing up.

Hot spots: High Head, Pilgrim Heights, Provincetown, 42.0563031 / -70.1161194; Corn Hill, Truro, 42.0061611 / -70.076766; Chapin Beach, Dennis, 41.730314 / -70.2350271; Sandy Neck Beach, Barnstable, 41.7391369 / -70.3801775; Scusset Beach State Reservation, Sagamore Beach, 41.7781927 / -70.500555

STARLING

EUROPEAN STARLING
Sturnus vulgaris

This introduced species arrived in North America in the 1800s and is now one of the most widespread and numerous birds on the continent.

Field marks: Starlings have three distinct plumages. Breeding adult has iridescent purple head, black eye, yellow bill, greenish back, greenish-black breast and belly, spotted flanks, black wings and short black tail with feathers outlined in brown. Nonbreeding adult has black head with white edges of each feather; black back, breast, belly, and flanks covered with white spots; scaly brownish wings and tail. Juvenile is softly brownish-gray with a light gray throat, slightly darker wings.

Size: L: 8.5", WS: 15.5"–16"

Similar species: Purple martin is more uniformly blue-black, with no spots or feather details. Female red-winged blackbird is browner, with a heavily streaked breast and back.

Season: Year-round

Habitat: Very comfortable in residential and commercial areas and a frequent visitor to backyard feeders. Starlings gather in enormous flocks to overwinter, often crowding on utility wires at busy intersections.

Food source: Omnivorous scavengers, starlings eat insects, invertebrates, spiders, fruit, berries, plants, and seeds offered at feeders, as well as human discards.

Nest: In a tree cavity, in a hole in a building, in a nest box, or in a hole excavated by woodpeckers

Call: Most often a high-pitched, descending *zheeer, zheeer*; a long, chattering phrase of syllables gleaned from other birds' songs. Starlings also have a rasping, nonmusical, one-note *hashhh* call to signify danger.

Hot spots: Any gathering place for people has a population of starlings, whether it's in the middle of a town or along an open beach. Look for them around the edges of shopping malls, on streets, at outdoor festivals, along the paths of electrical lines, and in your own backyard if you feed birds regularly. Starlings often form colonies of tens of thousands of birds in winter to scavenge for food together, creating clouds of birds that move in unison to avoid predators (search "murmuration" on YouTube for some astonishing examples). Such gatherings often are centered over a town, where warmth and activity attract the birds in the coldest months.

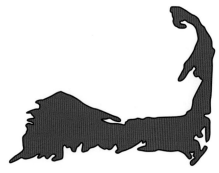

WAXWING

CEDAR WAXWING
Bombycilla cedrorum

An elegant year-round resident throughout New England, waxwings move among the treetops in flocks as they devour berries in winter and insects in all other seasons.

Field marks: Warm yellow-brown crest, neck, breast, and back; black mask outlined in white, white malar stripe against black throat, gray-brown upper wing, darker wing tips with red-tipped secondaries, lighter belly, white undertail coverts, black tail with yellow tip.

Size: L: 7"–7.25", WS: 11"–12"

Similar species: Bohemian waxwing is grayer overall, has white spots and yellow tips on its primaries, reddish undertail coverts, and a reddish forehead.

Season: Year-round

Habitat: Woodlands, neighborhoods, arboretums, orchards and other areas with many fruit trees

Food source: Insects, caterpillars, berries, fruit, sap, some flowers

Nest: On a branch in a tree with plenty of leaf canopy

Call: A single, high-pitched *pseeet*, often repeated

Hot spots: Any tall tree covered in berries in winter is likely to attract cedar waxwings, whether it's in a forest, an arboretum, or your backyard. Waxwings forage in flocks, sometimes with dozens or even hundreds of birds arriving together and blanketing a mountain ash or serviceberry tree. Listen for the high, piercing notes from many birds at once, and you will have no trouble spotting these handsome birds as they arrive.

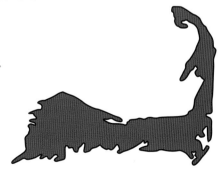

WARBLERS

YELLOW WARBLER
Setophaga petechia

America's most numerous and widespread warbler—with an estimated population of 39 million birds—is also one of its most delightful, with its cheery song and showy plumage.

Field marks: Male has bright yellow head, dull yellow back and tail, black eye and bill, yellow breast and underside with bright reddish streaks, light olive wings with black-outlined flight feathers. Female is very similar but lacks the red streaks.

Size: L: 5", WS: 7.75"–8"

Similar species: Prothonotary warbler has no red streaks, and its wings are blue-gray. American goldfinch is lemon yellow with a black cap and black wings.

Season: Spring migration; summer south of Wellfleet

Habitat: A combination of mixed woodlands and water features, including bogs, marshes, and swamps; also open fields, thickets, and residential areas

Food source: Insects, spiders, berries in a pinch

Nest: On a branch in a young tree

Call: A high-pitched warble, popularly parsed as *sweet-sweet-sweet-sweedle-sweet*; also a series of simple *tsp* notes when alarmed

Hot spots: Yellow warblers are easy to find in virtually any area with trees. Here are some spots with higher concentrations: Beech Forest, Provincetown, 42.0670802 / -70.1953679; Fort Hill, Eastham, 41.818792 / -69.9644995; Pogorelc Sanctuary, Barnstable, 41.699604 / -70.355493; Bell's Neck Conservation Area, West Harwich, 41.6840342 / -70.1129007; Santuit Pond, Mashpee, 41.6552018 / -70.4597425

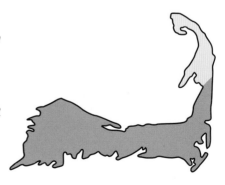

PRAIRIE WARBLER
Setophaga discolor

Listen before you look for this little yellow bird. It often gives away its location with its distinctive, steadily rising song.

Field marks: Male has olive head with yellow face, black eye line, black line from bill to below the eye, yellow throat and breast, black shoulder line, black streaks on yellow flanks, olive underside to white undertail coverts, olive back with rufous streaks, olive wings with faint yellow wing bars, olive tail. Female has olive face with a white patch above and below the eye, fainter black streaks on its flanks.

Size: L: 4.75", WS: 7"–7.5"

Similar species: Pine warbler has an olive head with yellow spectacles, olive streaks on its flanks, and gray wings. Female Cape May warbler has a gray face, back, and wings. Yellow warbler has an unmarked yellow face and red streaks on its breast and flanks; female has a clear yellow breast and flanks.

Season: Spring and fall migration; summer

Habitat: Open grasslands, including wetlands, pastures, farm fields, pine barrens, and scrubby woods

Food source: Insects

Nest: Near the ground in a small tree or shrub

Call: A rapid, emphatic *ziziziz/ziziZEEZEEZEEZEE,* rising steadily in pitch

Hot spots: Marconi Station Site, Wellfleet, 41.9140224 / -69.9714196; Fort Hill, Eastham, 41.818792 / -69.9644995; Monomoy National Wildlife Refuge, Chatham, 41.6568485 / -69.9582152; Chapin Beach, Dennis, 41.730314 / -70.2350271; Cape Cod Organic Farm, Barnstable, 41.6979064 / -70.2887732

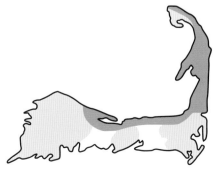

PALM WARBLER
Setophaga palmarum

This red-capped harbinger of spring is one of the first warblers to arrive each year, usually in the company of pine warblers.

Field marks: Breeding adult has bright rufous cap, yellow eyebrow, grayish-brown face with black eye line, small black bill, yellow throat, tan back and wings, yellow breast and underside with red streaks, yellow undertail coverts, tan tail. Fall (nonbreeding) adult has brown head with yellow eyebrow, whitish throat, dull underside with yellow wash, yellow undertail coverts; brown back, wings, and tail.

Size: L: 5.5", WS: 8"

Similar species: Yellow warbler has clear yellow face and head and yellow-olive back. Cape May warbler has bright orange patch on face and black streaks on underside.

Season: Spring and fall migration

Habitat: Open fields, wetland edges, beach scrubland

Food source: Insects

Nest: On the ground under a tree, in a clump of weeds and grass

Call: An unmusical trill, much like a cicada song but short

Hot spots: Beech Forest, Provincetown, 42.0670802 / -70.1953679; Wellfleet Bay Wildlife Sanctuary, Wellfleet, 41.8825315 / -69.995712; Fort Hill, Eastham, 41.818792 / -69.9644995; Harwich Community Garden, Harwich, 41.6746909 / -70.0910568; Frances A. Crane Wildlife Management Area, East Falmouth, 41.6348031 / -70.5607738

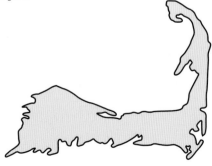

PINE WARBLER
Setophaga pinus

Pine forests erupt with the musical song of this early migrant in spring.

Field marks: Male has olive head and face with yellow spectacles, yellow dot above bill, yellow throat and breast, olive streaks on breast and flanks, white belly and undertail coverts, olive back, gray wings with two white wing bars, gray tail. Female lacks the streaking on breast, but has light streaks on flanks. Fall plumage: Gray head and back with white eye ring, pale neck patch, light gray underside with indistinct streaks on flanks, gray wings with white wing bars.

Size: L: 5.5", WS: 8.75"

Similar species: Female Cape May warbler has more distinct dark streaks on the breast and underside. Fall Cape May lacks the eye ring and has a greenish rump. Fall blackburnian warbler has yellow throat.

Season: Spring through fall

Habitat: Mixed or coniferous forests with pine trees

Food source: Insects, seeds, fruit

Nest: At the end of a pine tree branch at least 20 feet up, hidden by needles

Call: A long, melodious trill, similar to a chipping sparrow but slower

Hot spots: Herring River, Wellfleet, 41.9348807 / -70.0597715; Atlantic White Cedar Swamp Trail, South Wellfleet, 41.9136631 / -69.9731684; Fort Hill, Eastham, 41.818792 / -69.9644995; Nickerson State Park, Brewster, 41.7540898 / -70.0206757; Scusset Beach State Reservation, Sagamore Beach, 41.7781927 / -70.500555

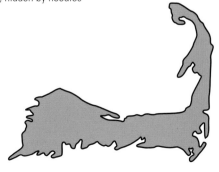

OVENBIRD
Seiurus aurocapilla

The best way to find this warbler is to follow its astonishingly loud teacher-teacher-teacher song. It gets its name from the oven-like shape of its nest.

Field marks: Orange crown stripe bordered by a black stripe on each side; light brown head, back, wings, and tail; large white eye ring, yellow bill, white throat with black vertical stripes, white underside with black streaks, light brown rear, white undertail coverts. Male, female, and nonbreeding plumages are all similar.

Size: L: 6", WS: 9.5"

Similar species: Wood thrush has a deep rufous head and back and is spotted rather than streaked on its underside. Swainson's thrush is larger, has a solid brown head and buff-yellow spectacles and is lightly spotted on its breast instead of streaked. Other thrushes are similarly spotted, with solid-color heads. Worm-eating warbler is smaller, has no streaking on its lower body, and has very thin black stripes on its head.

Season: Spring through fall

Habitat: Mature forests with open understory

Food source: Insects, worms, spiders, snails

Nest: On the ground, built like an oven to be entered from the side

Call: A loud, musical *teacher-teacher-teacher-teacher-teacher*, also a *whip, whip* chip note

Hot spots: Wellfleet Bay Wildlife Sanctuary, Wellfleet, 41.8825315 / -69.995712; Atlantic White Cedar Swamp Trail, South Wellfleet, 41.9136631 / -69.9731684; Nickerson State Park, Brewster, 41.7540898 / -70.0206757; Bell's Neck Conservation Area, West Harwich, 41.6840342 / -70.1129007; Santuit Pond, Mashpee, 41.6552018 / -70.4597425

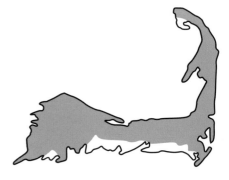

COMMON YELLOWTHROAT
Geothlypis trichas
"Common," in this case, is correct: Every wetland, forest pool, river, stream, lake, or bay on Cape Cod has some of these chatty, bright-colored warblers.

Field marks: Male has tan cap, nape, back, wings, and tail; black mask across eyes to the bill, extending to the throat on either side, with a white upper stripe; dark bill, yellow throat, tan belly and flanks, yellow undertail coverts. Female has tan head, neck, back, wings, tail, and underside; white eye ring, yellow throat and undertail coverts. *Fall plumage:* Male has tan head, back, wings, and tail; brown forehead, nearly black shading along the malars, yellow throat, tan underside, light yellow undertail coverts. Female is similar to male, but without the dark shading along the malar, and with a paler yellow throat.

Size: L: 5", WS: 6.75"

Similar species: Yellow-throated and yellow-rumped warblers have yellow throats, but with black and white heads and bodies. Magnolia warbler has a yellow throat and a black mask, but has a black and white head and body and heavy black streaks on its breast and underside.

Season: Summer

Habitat: Damp woods and fields, wetlands, streambeds, riparian areas, dunes near beaches, or along brushy road sides with drainage canals

Food source: Spiders, butterflies, dragonflies, beetles, grasshoppers, some seeds

Nest: Near the ground and concealed by high grasses and other vegetation

Call: A musical phrase with the common mnemonic *witchity, witchity, witchity, witt,* sometimes fast and sometimes slower; also a rapid, staccato trill like a rattlesnake and a general unmusical chatter

Hot spots: Any stop at a wetland, coastal dunes, forest edge near water, or a woodland bisected by a stream can yield at least one common yellowthroat. Listen for its song and calls to determine exactly where it might be, and watch for movement—yellowthroats are usually on the move through their habitat as they forage for food. These birds are also well known for responding to spishing, a birder trick to attract a bird's attention.

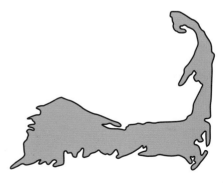

CARDINAL

NORTHERN CARDINAL
Cardinalis cardinalis

The denizen of backyard feeders and neighborhood parks throughout the eastern states, this local resident is one of the first birds that new birders recognize on sight.

Field marks: Male has bright red head with pronounced crest, black face, red bill, red body and tail with darker red wings. Female has brown body, crest with red wash, black face, bright orange bill, red wings and tail.

Size: L: 8.75", WS: 12"

Similar species: Scarlet tanager has no crest, has black wings and a black tail.

Season: Year-round

Habitat: Deciduous and coniferous woods, residential areas, woodland borders of farm fields and wetlands, parks

Food source: Seeds, insects, fruit, berries

Nest: In a bush or tree with low branches, not more than 5 feet from the ground

Call: Musical and varied, often beginning with a long, plunging pennywhistle note that ends with a *cha-cha-cha-cha-cha* series; or beginning with a *neerEET, neerEET* series and returning to the *cha-cha-cha* notes at the end. Other variations are likely. Also a metallic chip note, often heard just before dusk.

Hot spots: Every neighborhood has several families of cardinals, so you don't need to look far to find them. Draw them into your yard by offering black oil sunflower seed at your feeders, or take a walk in a park or on a converted rail trail to find them just beyond the first trees as you pass. Cardinals perch on the tops of fences or on posts as well as on low tree branches.

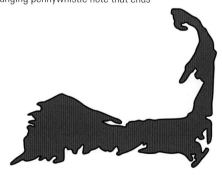

SPARROWS AND THEIR ALLIES

EASTERN TOWHEE
Pipilo erythrophthalmus

The East's only towhee (formerly known as rufous-sided) prefers to perch on top of stalks in open fields near woodlands.

Field marks: Male has black head, breast, back, wings, and tail; red eye, white underside, bright rufous flanks, light orange undertail coverts, white patch at the edge of the primary feathers. Female is identical to the male, but with a brown head, breast, back, wings, and tail instead of black.

Size: L: 7.5"–8.5", WS: 10.5"–11"

Similar species: American robin has a brown head, back, wings, and tail; a rufous underside from breast to belly. Rose-breasted grosbeak has a bright red breast.

Season: Spring through fall

Habitat: Open woods on the edges of brushy fields, especially among oak trees

Food source: Insects, seeds, berries, acorns

Nest: Under a dense shrub on the ground

Call: Commonly transcribed as *drink-your-TEEEEEEE*, two or three notes followed by a high, musical trill; also a rising *jeWINK* call note

Hot spots: Bridge Creek Conservation Area, Barnstable, 41.6996407 / -70.3741264; Sandy Neck Beach, Barnstable, 41.7391369 / -70.3801775; Hawksnest State Park, Harwich, 41.7092528 / -70.0439358; Monomoy National Wildlife Refuge, Chatham, 41.6568485 / -69.9582152; Marconi Station Site, Wellfleet, 41.9140224 / -69.9714196

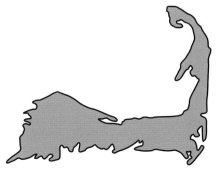

WHITE-THROATED SPARROW
Zonotrichia albicollis

If you don't see this bird at your backyard feeder, look for it on the forest floor, turning over leaves in search of seeds and bugs.

Field marks: Black and white–striped cap, yellow lores, gray face and bill, white throat edged in black, gray breast and underside, brown wings with two thin white wing bars, brown tail. Young lack the bright white cap and throat.

Size: L: 6.75"–7.75", WS: 9"–10"

Similar species: White-crowned sparrow has a gray throat, a pink bill, and no yellow on its face.

Season: Fall, winter and early spring

Habitat: Mixed woods with open understory, parks, gardens, backyards

Food source: Maple and oak leaf buds, seeds, insects

Nest: On or just above the ground, in a wooded area or in brush along a roadside or power line right-of-way

Call: Thready, musical song often transcribed as *old-sam-peabody-peabody-peabody*; also a sharp *chik* note

Hot spots: Great Sippewissett Marsh and Black Beach, Falmouth, 41.5890703 / -70.6442209; Cape Cod Organic Farm, Barnstable, 41.6979064 / -70.2887732; Fort Hill, Eastham, 41.818792 / -69.9644995; Herring River, Wellfleet, 41.9348807 / -70.0597715; High Head, Pilgrim Heights, Provincetown, 42.0563031 / -70.1161194

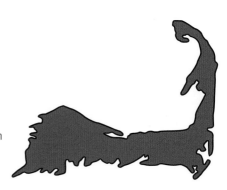

SONG SPARROW
Melospiza melodia

There are many variations in the song sparrow's appearance across the United States. The dark brown sparrows found on Cape Cod come from the Eastern race.

Field marks: Dark brown crown with a gray stripe up the middle, which sometimes stands up like a crest; gray eyebrow and cheek, brown eye line and malar stripe, white throat and chest, dark brown streaks on chest and flanks, culminating in a dark breast spot; gray back with brown stripes, brown and rufous wings and tail.

Size: L: 6.25", WS: 8.25"

Similar species: Fox sparrow is larger, plumper, and redder, with more flank streaks. Savannah sparrow has a yellow stripe over the eye, and its bill and tail are shorter. Lincoln's sparrow has finer streaking overall, a lighter-colored back, and a buff wash over its breast.

Season: Year-round

Habitat: Woodland edges, brushy fields, stands of thick shrubs, open wetlands, marshes, beach dunes, parks, gardens, backyard feeders

Food source: Seeds, berries, grasses, some insects

Nest: On the ground, usually surrounded by taller grass or weeds

Call: A varied series of rising and falling warbles, usually ending in a trill; also a high-pitched *seet*, sometimes followed by a single, much lower *hup* note

Hot spots: Virtually every open field, forest edge, and neighborhood has resident song sparrows. Detectable first by song, they often pop up to stand at the top of a small shrub or on a blade of tall grass and sing, throwing their heads back and pumping out the notes using their entire bodies for emphasis. These sparrows are easy to spot and cooperative in giving birders good looks.

SWAMP SPARROW
Melospiza georgiana

With its bright rufous or brown cap and a song similar to a chipping sparrow, the swamp sparrow can be easy to confuse with a chipping—but habitat decreases the margin for error.

Field marks: Male has bright rufous cap, gray face, black patch at ear, buff malars, white throat, gray underside with rufous flanks; rufous and black back, wings, and tail. Female is the same except with a dark brown cap.

Size: L: 5.75", WS: 7.25"

Similar species: Lincoln's sparrow has a dark brown cap with a gray central stripe, a buff breast streaked with black. Chipping sparrow is slightly smaller and has a bright white eyebrow, white malars, and a less rufous back.

Season: Winter; spring and fall migration closer to the mainland

Habitat: Saltwater and freshwater wetlands and swamps with tall grasses and reeds

Food source: Grasshoppers, crickets, ants, and other insects; seeds

Nest: Constructed over water in a mass of vegetation

Call: A continuous trill, sometimes quite rapid, sometimes slow and whistled; also a simple *chik* call note

Hot spots: Sandy Neck Beach, Barnstable, 41.7391369 / -70.3801775; Bell's Neck Conservation Area, West Harwich, 41.6840342 / -70.1129007; Fort Hill, Eastham, 41.818792 / -69.9644995; Wellfleet Bay Wildlife Sanctuary, Wellfleet, 41.8825315 / -69.995712; Pochet Island, Orleans, 41.7670547 / -69.9404669

HOUSE SPARROW
Passer domesticus

No household is complete without a dozen or so of these in the backyard. This introduced species from England can be found anywhere that humans frequent, from front porches to town squares.

Field marks: Male has gray cap, wide brown stripe from eye to back, gray cheek; black eye, bill, throat, and breast; white collar, gray belly and flanks, brown back, brown and black wings, white patch on wing, gray tail. Female is drab grayish tan overall with small yellow bill, thin white eye line, brown and gray wings with thin white wing bar, brown tail.

Size: L: 6.25", WS: 9.5"

Similar species: No other Cape Cod bird has the facial pattern of a male house sparrow.

Season: Year-round

Habitat: Towns, parks, neighborhoods, backyards with bird feeders

Food source: Seeds, fruit, crumbs from human discards, some insects

Nest: In a tree cavity, a hole in a building, a bowl created by a man-made sign, or a man-made nest box. House sparrows are known to evict eastern bluebirds from nest boxes and take them over for their own broods.

Call: A simple, fairly dry *cheep* from a male and a chattier series of *cheeps* from a female are familiar sounds in most neighborhoods.

Hot spots: This ubiquitous sparrow is found in every backyard, park, garden, beach, street, outdoor restaurant, and even inside big-box stores and malls, where they plunder the crumbs humans leave behind in food courts. No hot spot is required to find a house sparrow; chances are you can see one outside your window as you read this.

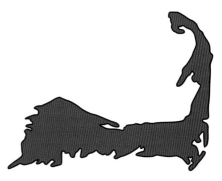

JUNCO

DARK-EYED JUNCO
Junco hyemalis

If you travel across the country, you'll encounter this bird in as many as six different plumages. Juncos on Cape Cod are the "slate-colored" variety.

Field marks: Male is solid slate gray above, with pink bill, white belly, gray rear, white undertail coverts, gray tail with white outer feathers. Female has slate gray head, breast, and back; gray wings with some brown feathers, white belly, gray rear, white undertail coverts, gray tail with white outer feathers.

Size: L: 5.75"–6.25", WS: 9.25"–10"

Similar species: Tufted titmouse has a gray crest, nape, back, and wings; a white throat, breast, and belly; and rosy flanks. Eastern towhee is larger and has a black head, white underside, and bright rust-orange flanks.

Season: Winter, with some concentrations in early spring and late fall

Habitat: Woodland edges, neighborhoods, parks, gardens, fields with adjacent woodlands, roadsides

Food source: Seeds, insects, fruit, berries

Nest: On the ground or just above it, in a shrub or brush pile, or under a log

Call: High, full-bodied, three-second trill, sometimes broken halfway through

Hot spots: Widespread and numerous, juncos inhabit just about every wooded area on Cape Cod throughout the winter. Look for them along quiet roadsides as they search for grit. Juncos also feed on the ground under bird feeders and on platform feeders filled with sunflower seed.

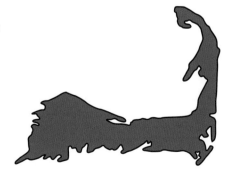

BLACKBIRDS AND ORIOLE

BROWN-HEADED COWBIRD
Molothrus ater

Cowbirds are notorious in the birding world for laying their eggs in the nests of other birds, abandoning their babies for others to raise.

Field marks: Male has brown head, black body with a slightly turquoise sheen. Female is uniformly drab gray-brown, with slightly darker wings.

Size: L: 7.5", WS: 12"

Similar species: Rusty blackbird is uniformly blue-black with a yellow eye. Common grackle has an iridescent blue head, a blackish body, and a very long tail.

Season: Summer

Habitat: Edges of wooded areas, farm fields, neighborhoods, parks

Food source: Insects, seeds

Nest: Lays one egg per nest of another bird species. In one season, a single cowbird may lay as many as thirty-six eggs in other birds' nests.

Call: A liquid-sounding burble, ending in a very high squeal: *blug-lug-EET*

Hot spots: Find cowbirds in just about any green space, especially those with open fields adjacent to forest edges. These birds usually move and feed in flocks, so if you discover one cowbird, you are likely to see many more.

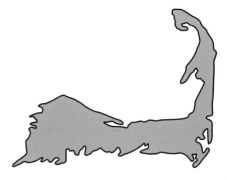

RED-WINGED BLACKBIRD

Agelaius phoeniceus

No open field or beach edge is complete without a colony of these highly visible, always active blackbirds.

Field marks: Male is solid black from head to tail, with a red and yellow patch at the shoulder. Female is like a large sparrow, with a brown cap, lighter brown eyebrow and malar stripe, brown cheek, buff under-side streaked with dark brown, brown wings with two white wing bars, brown tail.

Size: L: 8.75"–9.5", WS: 13"–14.5"

Similar species: Rusty blackbird, common grackle, European starling, and brown-headed cowbird have no wing patch. Female rose-breasted grosbeak has a more vivid facial pattern than female red-winged blackbird and more finely streaked underparts and a yellow patch under each wing.

Season: Spring migration and summer

Habitat: Open fields, meadows, wetlands of all varieties, beach dunes, woodland edges, neighborhoods

Food source: Insects, seeds, fruit, marine invertebrates, crop grains; red-wings also come to backyard feeders.

Nest: Firmly attached to reeds or other canes in grassy marshes or other wetlands

Call: A familiar three-note *onk-or-REE*; also a piercing, descending whistle and a deeper descending trill

Hot spots: Any plot of land with tall grasses contains red-winged blackbirds from April through September, whether it's in an agricultural area, a wildlife refuge, in a creek near a shopping mall, along a drainage ditch on a roadside, or alongside a schoolyard. Red-wings perch on top of cattails and phragmites, hop through low shrubs and the lowest branches of trees on woodland edges, and show up at backyard feeders when natural food sources become scarce.

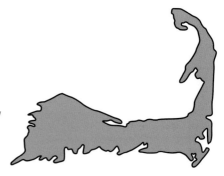

COMMON GRACKLE
Quiscalus quiscula

The grackle's long, rudder-shaped tail makes it easy to differentiate from cowbirds and blackbirds.

Field marks: Blue-black, iridescent head and breast, yellow eye, large black bill, uniformly brown-black body, long tail with flat, triangular end.

Size: L: 12.5"–13.5", WS: 17"–18.5"

Similar species: Rusty blackbird is blue-black all over and has a shorter tail. Red-winged blackbird is smaller, has a red and yellow patch on its wings, and has a shorter tail. European starling is smaller, with a short tail.

Season: Spring through early fall

Habitat: City streets, parks, and neighborhoods; meadows, fields, beaches, dunes, shrubby areas

Food source: Insects, seeds, fish, fruit, eggs and nestlings in other birds' nests

Nest: Up to 12 feet off the ground in a tree or tall shrub

Call: An unmusical *chaa-ak, chaa-REE*, like the creak of metal against metal

Hot spots: All it takes to find a common grackle is a walk down any town or suburban street, a stroll through a beach parking lot or along a shopping center's edges, or a scan of the trees near an open field. Grackles often crowd other birds off backyard feeders (especially the platform variety), and they have been known to peck the head of a house sparrow until the smaller bird relinquishes a prime feeder perch.

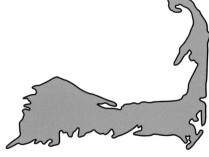

BALTIMORE ORIOLE
Icterus galbula

Perhaps the most hoped-for backyard bird, this stunningly orange and black creature comes readily to feeders that offer oranges and grape jelly.

Field marks: Male has black head, throat, and back; orange breast and underside, black wings with orange patches at shoulder and one white wing bar, orange lower back and rump, black tail with orange outer feathers. Female has yellow-orange head and body with patchy black pattern on head, white throat, black wings with white wing bars, paler yellow flanks, yellow-orange rump and tail. Nonbreeding male has dull yellow head; bright yellow-orange throat, breast, underside, undertail coverts, and tail; pale flanks, black wings with white wing bars.

Size: L: 8.75", WS: 11.5"

Similar species: American robin has a brown head, white eye ring, brown back and wings, reddish-orange breast, and white undertail coverts. Eastern towhee has a black head and white breast and underside, with dark orange streaks on flanks. Orchard oriole is similar but with a darker, burnt-orange body.

Season: Summer

Habitat: Wooded areas, parks, gardens, suburban backyards with mature trees

Food source: Caterpillars, moths, fruit, flower nectar; also hummingbird nectar, oranges, and grape jelly from backyard feeders

Nest: In a tree in a woven basket nest, usually more than 20 feet from the ground

Call: A syrupy, musical series of clearly defined, whistled notes: *hee-doo-HEE-dee-doo-dee-hoo* and variations of this; also a simple *peep* note, followed by a descending whistle (like a pennywhistle)

Hot spots: How can a bird so beautiful be so common? Baltimore orioles can be found in just about any suburban neighborhood with mature trees. Woodlands can be full of them during migration, but orioles quickly establish territory and go about the business of searching for bugs, fruit, nectar, and jelly feeders to keep their energy up during the breeding season. They may disappear from your feeders for a few weeks as they raise their young, but they will return with their fledglings later in the summer.

FINCHES

HOUSE FINCH
Haemorhous mexicanus

This small, long-tailed finch came from the western United States and found its way here through New York City pet stores in the 1940s. Today it is the most widespread finch in the region.

Field marks: Male has red forehead, face, throat, breast, and rump; pale gray nape, white underside with gray streaks and a pink wash, black wings with thin white wing bars, long dark tail. Female has drab gray-brown head, throat, and back; light gray breast and underside with darker gray streaks, dark wings with two slim white wing bars, gray tail.

Size: L: 6", WS: 9.5"–10"

Similar species: Purple finch is more uniformly pink overall. Red and white-winged crossbills are a deeper red from head to tail.

Season: Year-round

Habitat: Neighborhoods, cities, parks, gardens, arboretums, backyards with feeders

Food source: Seeds, fruit

Nest: In a tree cavity, deep in a shrub, or in a crack or hole in a building

Call: Continuous, often lengthy series of warbles, whistles, trills, and chatter

Hot spots: Every neighborhood has at least a small flock of house finches, especially if some of the residents keep their seed feeders stocked. House finches are particularly easy to see from late summer through winter, when they bring their fledglings to feeders and birdbaths. They often flock together in a single large shrub a short distance from a ready food source.

AMERICAN GOLDFINCH
Spinus tristis
The only all-yellow bird with black wings in the United States, this goldfinch is a regular visitor to backyards, gardens, and parks in every season.

Field marks: Male has black forehead; yellow head, back, upper wings, throat, breast, and underside; pink bill, black wings with one white wing bar, white rump, black tail. Female has olive-gray head, yellow eye ring, yellow throat, dull yellow breast and flanks with indistinct olive-gray streaks, olive-gray back, black wings with one white and one buff wing bar, white patch under the wing, white undertail and rump, black tail. *Fall plumage:* Male has gray head, back, and underside; yellow patch around eye, gray bill, yellow throat, yellow shoulders, black wings with one whitish wing bar, black tail. Female is uniformly drab brownish-gray with black wings, one brownish wing bar, white undertail, black tail with whitish edges.

Size: L: 5", WS: 9"

Similar species: Yellow warbler is yellow overall, with red streaks on its breast and flanks. Prothonotary warbler is uniformly golden-yellow with gray-blue wings.

Season: Year-round

Habitat: Open grassland, marshes, thickets, woodland edges, beach scrub, neighborhoods, parks, gardens

Food source: Seeds, particularly from flower heads; nyjer and sunflower seeds at feeders

Nest: In a shrub or young tree, not far from the ground

Call: A simple, lilting *twee-twee-twee-twee-twee*; also a rising *per-WEE* alarm call and a rapid, descending *DEE-dee-dee-dee* in flight

Hot spots: Goldfinches are one of the most common birds on Cape Cod, found in virtually every grassy area, from the vacant lot behind a shopping center to the national seashore. They are frequent visitors to feeders, often commandeering a nyjer feeder and feeding in small flocks from every port. In summer, watch fields of coneflowers, black-eyed Susans, and teasel for perching goldfinches pulling seeds from the flower heads.

APPENDIX A: SPECIES BY COLOR

This list contains all of the birds you may see on Cape Cod, as listed in appendix B. Some of these birds are not pictured in this book; our *Birding New England* provides photos of all these birds to help you identify the less common ones.

Birds with Pink or Red Plumage

Canvasback
Redhead
Red-headed woodpecker
Red-bellied woodpecker
Yellow-bellied sapsucker
Ruby-crowned kinglet
Ruby-throated hummingbird
Red-winged blackbird
Hermit thrush
Scarlet tanager
Northern cardinal
Pine grosbeak
Rose-breasted grosbeak
Purple finch
House finch
Red crossbill
White-winged crossbill

Birds with Orange or Rufous Plumage

Horned grebe
Northern shoveler
Ruddy duck
Common merganser (female)
Red-breasted merganser
Green heron
Virginia rail
King rail
Clapper rail
Ruddy turnstone
Red knot
Hudsonian godwit
Red phalarope
Cooper's hawk
Red-tailed hawk
American kestrel
Great-crested flycatcher
Barn swallow
Brown thrasher

Eastern bluebird
American robin
Wood thrush
Chestnut-sided warbler
Bay-breasted warbler
Blackburnian warbler
American redstart
Baltimore oriole
Orchard oriole
Eastern towhee
Fox sparrow
Song sparrow
Nelson's sparrow
Saltmarsh sparrow

Birds with Yellow Plumage

Great-crested flycatcher
Yellow-bellied flycatcher
Horned lark
Philadelphia vireo
Yellow-throated vireo
Northern parula
Yellow-throated warbler
Black-throated green warbler
Prothonotary warbler
Magnolia warbler
Yellow-rumped warbler
Canada warbler
Cape May warbler
Chestnut-sided warbler
Blackburnian warbler (female)
American redstart (female)
Pine warbler
Prairie warbler
Palm warbler
Blue-winged warbler
Yellow warbler
Wilson's warbler
Hooded warbler

Nashville warbler
Mourning warbler
Common yellowthroat
Eastern meadowlark
Orchard oriole (female)
Baltimore oriole (female)
Scarlet tanager (female)
Dickcissel
Red crossbill (female)
American goldfinch
Evening grosbeak

Birds with Green or Olive Plumage

Wood duck
Mallard
Northern shoveler
Green-winged teal
American wigeon
Greater scaup
Common goldeneye
Common merganser
Red-breasted merganser
Green heron
Ruby-throated hummingbird
Rufous hummingbird
Ruby-crowned kinglet
Golden-crowned kinglet
Yellow-throated vireo
Blue-headed vireo
Black-throated green warbler
Pine warbler
Prairie warbler
Tennessee warbler
Orange-crowned warbler
Nashville warbler
Mourning warbler
Scarlet tanager (female)

Birds with Blue or Iridescent Plumage

Snow goose, "blue" phase
Blue-winged teal
Harlequin duck
Ruddy duck (blue bill in breeding plumage)
Belted kingfisher
Purple martin

Cliff swallow
Barn swallow
Tree swallow
Blue jay
Blue-gray gnatcatcher
Eastern bluebird
Blue-headed vireo
Prothonotary warbler
Black-throated blue warbler
Cerulean warbler
Blue-winged warbler
Common grackle
European starling
Indigo bunting

Birds with Purple Plumage

Lesser scaup
Glossy ibis
Purple martin
Common grackle
European starling

Birds with Predominantly Brown Plumage

Horned grebe
Pied-billed grebe
Canada goose
American black duck
Mallard (female)
Gadwall (female)
Common pintail (female)
American wigeon (female)
Eurasian wigeon (female)
Wood duck (female)
Northern shoveler (female)
Blue-winged teal (female)
Green-winged teal (female)
White-winged scoter (female)
Black scoter (female)
Surf scoter (female)
King eider (female)
Common eider (female)
Canvasback (female)
Redhead (female)
Ring-necked duck (female)
Lesser scaup (female)

Greater scaup (female)
Common goldeneye (female)
Barrow's goldeneye (female)
Bufflehead (female)
Ruddy duck (female)
Hooded merganser (female)
Common gallinule
Leach's storm-petrel
American bittern
Least bittern
Sandhill crane
Virginia rail
King rail
Clapper rail
Sora
American oystercatcher
Black-bellied plover (winter)
American golden-plover
Ruddy turnstone (winter)
Semipalmated plover
Piping plover
Killdeer
American woodcock
Short-billed dowitcher
Long-billed dowitcher
Red knot
Hudsonian godwit
Marbled godwit
Whimbrel
Sanderling
Buff-breasted sandpiper
Upland sandpiper
Pectoral sandpiper
Ruff
Stilt sandpiper
Dunlin
Spotted sandpiper
Least sandpiper
Semipalmated sandpiper
Baird's sandpiper
Western sandpiper
White-rumped sandpiper
Wild turkey
Ring-necked pheasant
Ruffed grouse
Spruce grouse (female)

Northern bobwhite
Northern harrier (female)
Red-tailed hawk
Rough-legged hawk
Red-shouldered hawk
Broad-winged hawk
Bald eagle
Osprey
Turkey vulture
Merlin (female)
Short-eared owl
Long-eared owl
Great horned owl
Barred owl
Northern saw-whet owl
Mourning dove
Yellow-billed cuckoo
Black-billed cuckoo
Common nighthawk
Eastern whip-poor-will
Northern flicker
Horned lark
American pipit
Bank swallow
Northern rough-winged swallow
Brown creeper
House wren
Winter wren
Carolina wren
Marsh wren
Sedge wren
Brown thrasher
American robin
Hermit thrush
Swainson's thrush
Gray-cheeked thrush
Bicknell's thrush
Veery
Cedar waxwing
Bohemian waxwing
Worm-eating warbler
Northern waterthrush
Louisiana waterthrush
Ovenbird
Brown-headed cowbird
Bobolink (female)

Eastern meadowlark
Dickcissel
Lapland longspur
Snow bunting (winter)
Northern cardinal (female)
Common redpoll
Pine siskin
Rose-breasted grosbeak (female)
Eastern towhee (female)
White-throated sparrow
White-crowned sparrow
Chipping sparrow
Field sparrow
Clay-colored sparrow
American tree sparrow
Swamp sparrow
Lark sparrow
Grasshopper sparrow
Henslow's sparrow
Vesper sparrow
Fox sparrow
Song sparrow
Lincoln's sparrow
Nelson's sparrow
Saltmarsh sparrow
Seaside sparrow

Birds with Predominantly Black Plumage

Common loon
Red-throated loon
Razorbill
Common murre
Thick-billed murre
Atlantic puffin
Dovekie
Black guillemot
Great cormorant
Double-crested cormorant
White-winged scoter
Surf scoter
Black scoter
Long-tailed duck
King eider
Common eider
Ring-necked duck

Common goldeneye
Barrow's goldeneye
Hooded merganser
American coot
Great shearwater
Cory's shearwater
Sooty shearwater
Manx shearwater
Wilson's storm-petrel
Parasitic jaeger
Pomarine jaeger
Great black-backed gull
Lesser black-backed gull
Black tern
Black skimmer
Black-crowned night-heron
Black-necked stilt
American avocet
Black-bellied plover
American golden-plover
Spruce grouse
Black vulture
Pileated woodpecker
Red-headed woodpecker
Red-bellied woodpecker
Yellow-bellied sapsucker
Black-backed woodpecker
American three-toed woodpecker
Downy woodpecker
Hairy woodpecker
Eastern kingbird
Chimney swift
American crow
Fish crow
Common raven
Black-and-white warbler
Blackpoll warbler
Blackburnian warbler
American redstart
Red-winged blackbird
Brown-headed cowbird
Rusty blackbird
Common grackle
European starling
Rose-breasted grosbeak
Eastern towhee

Birds with Predominantly Gray Plumage

Red-necked grebe (winter)
Greater white-fronted goose
Brant
Gadwall
Common pintail
Green-winged teal
Canvasback
Redhead
Greater scaup
Lesser scaup
Common merganser (female)
Red-breasted merganser (female)
Hooded merganser (female)
Northern fulmar
Herring gull
Ring-billed gull
Black-legged kittiwake
Laughing gull
Bonaparte's gull
Least tern
Arctic tern
Common tern
Roseate tern
Forster's tern
Black-crowned night-heron
Yellow-crowned night-heron
Willet
Lesser yellowlegs
Greater yellowlegs
Stilt sandpiper
Wilson's phalarope
Sanderling (winter)
Dunlin (winter)
Purple sandpiper
Least sandpiper (winter)
Semipalmated sandpiper (winter)
Western sandpiper (winter)
Baird's sandpiper (winter)
White-rumped sandpiper (winter)
Red-necked phalarope (winter)
Red phalarope (winter)
Sharp-shinned hawk
Cooper's hawk

Northern goshawk
Northern harrier
Merlin
Peregrine falcon
Eastern screech-owl
Great gray owl
Rock pigeon
Eastern phoebe
Eastern wood-pewee
Olive-sided flycatcher
Acadian flycatcher
Yellow-bellied flycatcher
Least flycatcher
Willow flycatcher
Alder flycatcher
Canada jay
Black-capped chickadee
Tufted titmouse
White-breasted nuthatch
Red-breasted nuthatch
Gray catbird
Northern mockingbird
Northern shrike
Bohemian waxwing
Northern parula
Yellow-throated warbler
Magnolia warbler
Yellow-rumped warbler
Canada warbler
Golden-winged warbler
Dark-eyed junco
Pine grosbeak (female)
Seaside sparrow

Birds with Predominantly White Plumage

Mute swan
Tundra swan
Snow goose
Common eider
King eider
Common goldeneye
Barrow's goldeneye
Bufflehead
American white pelican
Northern gannet

Glaucous gull
Iceland gull
Herring gull
Ring-billed gull
Black-legged kittiwake
Great black-backed gull
Lesser black-backed gull
Royal tern
Caspian tern
Least tern
Arctic tern

Common tern
Forster's tern
Great egret
Snowy egret
White ibis
Black-necked stilt
American avocet
Barn owl
Snowy owl
Snow bunting

APPENDIX B: A REALISTIC CHECKLIST OF THE BIRDS OF CAPE COD

The following checklist is compiled from the official bird checklists of the Cape Cod Bird Club and from Mass Audubon for its wildlife sanctuaries on the Cape Cod peninsula. The original checklists each included rare species not regularly seen here, as well as accidentals—birds very far from their native habitat, brought here by storms or other forces of nature—and species that are extirpated from the region or believed to be extinct. We have omitted these accidental birds to help you set realistic expectations for the birds you are most likely to see on an average day in the proper habitat, season, and time of day. Should some surprising birds make an appearance, there's room at the end to write in these unusual sightings.

Loons
- ❐ Red-throated loon
- ❐ Common loon

Grebes
- ❐ Red-necked grebe
- ❐ Horned grebe
- ❐ Pied-billed grebe

Shearwaters
- ❐ Northern fulmar
- ❐ Great shearwater
- ❐ Cory's shearwater
- ❐ Sooty shearwater
- ❐ Manx shearwater

Storm-Petrels
- ❐ Wilson's storm-petrel
- ❐ Leach's storm-petrel

Gannet
- ❐ Northern gannet

Cormorants
- ❐ Great cormorant
- ❐ Double-crested cormorant

Herons, Egrets, and Bitterns
- ❐ American bittern
- ❐ Least bittern

- ❐ Great blue heron
- ❐ Great egret
- ❐ Snowy egret
- ❐ Tricolored heron
- ❐ Little blue heron
- ❐ Cattle egret
- ❐ Green heron
- ❐ Black-crowned night-heron
- ❐ Yellow-crowned night-heron
- ❐ Glossy ibis

Swan and Geese
- ❐ Mute swan
- ❐ Canada goose
- ❐ Brant
- ❐ Snow goose
- ❐ Ducks
- ❐ Wood duck
- ❐ Gadwall
- ❐ American wigeon
- ❐ Eurasian wigeon
- ❐ American black duck
- ❐ Mallard
- ❐ Blue-winged teal
- ❐ Northern shoveler
- ❐ Northern pintail
- ❐ Green-winged teal

☐ Canvasback
☐ Redhead
☐ Ring-necked duck
☐ Greater scaup
☐ Lesser scaup
☐ King eider
☐ Common eider
☐ Harlequin duck
☐ Surf scoter
☐ White-winged scoter
☐ Black scoter
☐ Long-tailed duck
☐ Bufflehead
☐ Common goldeneye
☐ Barrow's goldeneye
☐ Hooded merganser
☐ Common merganser
☐ Red-breasted merganser
☐ Ruddy duck

Ground Birds
☐ Northern bobwhite
☐ Ring-necked pheasant
☐ Ruffed grouse
☐ Wild turkey

Duck-like Birds
☐ American coot

Vultures
☐ Black vulture
☐ Turkey vulture

Osprey
☐ Osprey

Harrier
☐ Northern harrier

Eagle
☐ Bald eagle

Accipiters
☐ Sharp-shinned hawk
☐ Cooper's hawk
☐ Northern goshawk

Buteos
☐ Red-shouldered hawk
☐ Broad-winged hawk
☐ Red-tailed hawk
☐ Rough-legged hawk

Falcons
☐ Merlin
☐ American kestrel
☐ Peregrine falcon

Rails
☐ Sora
☐ Virginia rail
☐ Clapper rail

Plovers
☐ Black-bellied plover
☐ American golden-plover
☐ Piping plover
☐ Semipalmated plover
☐ Killdeer
☐ American oystercatcher

Sandpipers
☐ Spotted sandpiper
☐ Greater yellowlegs
☐ Willet
☐ Lesser yellowlegs
☐ Solitary sandpiper
☐ Upland sandpiper
☐ Whimbrel
☐ Hudsonian godwit
☐ Marbled godwit
☐ Ruddy turnstone
☐ Red knot
☐ Sanderling
☐ Semipalmated sandpiper
☐ Western sandpiper
☐ Least sandpiper
☐ White-rumped sandpiper
☐ Baird's sandpiper
☐ Pectoral sandpiper
☐ Purple sandpiper
☐ Dunlin

- ❏ Stilt sandpiper
- ❏ Buff-breasted sandpiper
- ❏ Short-billed dowitcher
- ❏ Long-billed dowitcher
- ❏ Wilson's snipe
- ❏ American woodcock
- ❏ Wilson's phalarope
- ❏ Red-necked phalarope
- ❏ Red phalarope

Gulls
- ❏ Laughing gull
- ❏ Little gull
- ❏ Black-headed gull
- ❏ Bonaparte's gull
- ❏ Ring-billed gull
- ❏ Herring gull
- ❏ Iceland gull
- ❏ Lesser black-backed gull
- ❏ Glaucous gull
- ❏ Great black-backed gull
- ❏ Sabine's gull
- ❏ Black-legged kittiwake

Terns
- ❏ Least tern
- ❏ Caspian tern
- ❏ Black tern
- ❏ Roseate tern
- ❏ Common tern
- ❏ Arctic tern
- ❏ Forster's tern
- ❏ Royal tern
- ❏ Sandwich tern
- ❏ Black skimmer

Jaegers
- ❏ Pomarine
- ❏ Parasitic

Auks (Alcids)
- ❏ Dovekie
- ❏ Common murre
- ❏ Thick-billed murre
- ❏ Razorbill

- ❏ Black guillemot

Dove and Pigeon
- ❏ Mourning dove
- ❏ Rock pigeon

Cuckoos
- ❏ Yellow-billed cuckoo
- ❏ Black-billed cuckoo

Owls
- ❏ Barn owl
- ❏ Eastern screech-owl
- ❏ Great horned owl
- ❏ Snowy owl
- ❏ Barred owl
- ❏ Short-eared owl
- ❏ Northern saw-whet owl

Nightjars
- ❏ Common nighthawk
- ❏ Eastern whip-poor-will
- ❏ Swift
- ❏ Chimney swift

Hummingbird
- ❏ Ruby-throated hummingbird

Kingfisher
- ❏ Belted kingfisher

Woodpeckers
- ❏ Red-headed woodpecker
- ❏ Red-bellied woodpecker
- ❏ Yellow-bellied sapsucker
- ❏ Downy woodpecker
- ❏ Hairy woodpecker
- ❏ Northern flicker

Flycatchers
- ❏ Olive-sided flycatcher
- ❏ Eastern wood-pewee
- ❏ Yellow-bellied flycatcher
- ❏ Acadian flycatcher
- ❏ Alder flycatcher
- ❏ Willow flycatcher
- ❏ Least flycatcher

❏ Eastern phoebe
❏ Great-crested flycatcher
❏ Eastern kingbird

Shrike
❏ Northern shrike

Vireos
❏ White-eyed vireo
❏ Yellow-throated vireo
❏ Blue-headed vireo
❏ Warbling vireo
❏ Philadelphia vireo
❏ Red-eyed vireo

Jay and Crows
❏ Blue jay
❏ American crow
❏ Fish crow

Lark
❏ Horned lark

Swallows
❏ Purple martin
❏ Tree swallow
❏ Northern rough-winged swallow
❏ Bank swallow
❏ Cliff swallow
❏ Barn swallow

Titmouse and Chickadee
❏ Tufted titmouse
❏ Black-capped chickadee

Nuthatches and Creeper
❏ Red-breasted nuthatch
❏ White-breasted nuthatch
❏ Brown creeper

Wrens
❏ Carolina wren
❏ House wren
❏ Winter wren
❏ Marsh wren

Kinglets and Gnatcatcher
❏ Golden-crowned kinglet

❏ Ruby-crowned kinglet
❏ Blue-gray gnatcatcher

Thrushes
❏ Eastern bluebird
❏ Veery
❏ Swainson's thrush
❏ Hermit thrush
❏ Wood thrush
❏ American robin

Mimic Thrushes
❏ Gray catbird
❏ Northern mockingbird
❏ Brown thrasher

Starling and Pipit
❏ European starling
❏ American pipit

Waxwings
❏ Bohemian waxwing
❏ Cedar waxwing

Warblers
❏ Blue-winged warbler
❏ Tennessee warbler
❏ Orange-crowned warbler
❏ Nashville warbler
❏ Northern parula
❏ Yellow warbler
❏ Chestnut-sided warbler
❏ Magnolia warbler
❏ Cape May warbler
❏ Black-throated blue warbler
❏ Yellow-rumped warbler
❏ Black-throated green warbler
❏ Blackburnian warbler
❏ Pine warbler
❏ Prairie warbler
❏ Palm warbler
❏ Bay-breasted warbler
❏ Blackpoll warbler
❏ Cerulean warbler
❏ Black-and-white warbler

❏ American redstart
❏ Prothonotary warbler
❏ Worm-eating warbler
❏ Ovenbird
❏ Northern waterthrush
❏ Kentucky warbler
❏ Connecticut warbler
❏ Mourning warbler
❏ Common yellowthroat
❏ Hooded warbler
❏ Wilson's warbler
❏ Canada warbler
❏ Yellow-breasted chat

Tanagers
❏ Summer tanager
❏ Scarlet tanager

Sparrows
❏ Eastern towhee
❏ American tree sparrow
❏ Chipping sparrow
❏ Clay-colored sparrow
❏ Field sparrow
❏ Vesper sparrow
❏ Lark sparrow
❏ Savannah sparrow
❏ Grasshopper sparrow
❏ Nelson's sparrow
❏ Saltmarsh sparrow
❏ Seaside sparrow
❏ Fox sparrow
❏ Song sparrow
❏ Lincoln's sparrow

❏ Swamp sparrow
❏ White-throated sparrow
❏ White-crowned sparrow

Sparrow Allies
❏ Dark-eyed junco
❏ Lapland longspur
❏ Snow bunting
❏ Northern cardinal
❏ Rose-breasted grosbeak
❏ Blue grosbeak
❏ Indigo bunting
❏ Dickcissel

Blackbirds
❏ Bobolink
❏ Red-winged blackbird
❏ Eastern meadowlark
❏ Rusty blackbird
❏ Common grackle
❏ Brown-headed cowbird
❏ Orchard oriole
❏ Baltimore oriole

Finches and Allies
❏ Pine grosbeak
❏ Purple finch
❏ House finch
❏ Red crossbill
❏ White-winged crossbill
❏ Common redpoll
❏ Pine siskin
❏ American goldfinch
❏ House sparrow

APPENDIX C: RESOURCES

"All About Birds." Cornell Laboratory of Ornithology, allaboutbirds.org.

"Bird Checklist for Felix Neck." Mass Audubon, accessed May 4, 2020, massaudubon .org/content/download/2651/28429/file/checklist_Felixneck.pdf.

"Bird Checklist for Wellfleet Bay." Mass Audubon, accessed May 4, 2020, massaudubon .org/content/download/2979/34037/file/wellfleet%20bird%20checklist.pdf.

"Birds of North America." Cornell Laboratory of Ornithology, birdsna.org/Species-Account/bna/home.

Dunn, Jon L., and Jonathan Alderfer. *Field Guide to the Birds of North America.* 7th ed. Washington, DC: National Geographic Society, September 12, 2017.

eBird (globally crowdsourced content). Cornell Laboratory of Ornithology, ebird.org.

"Massachusetts Avian Records Committee Official State List." Massachusetts Avian Records Committee, December 2017, maavianrecords.com/official-state-list/.

Nickerson, Colin. "New England Sees a Return of Forests, Wildlife." *Boston Globe*, August 31, 2013, accessed July 13, 2018, bostonglobe.com/metro/2013/08/31/new-england-sees-return-forests-and-wildlife/IJRxacvGcHeQDmtZt09WvN/story.html.

Nikula, Blair. "Checklist of the Birds of Cape Cod, Massachusetts." Cape Cod Bird Club, 2008, capecodbirds.org/CapeCodChecklist2008.pdf.

Peterson, Roger Tory. *A Field Guide to the Birds: A Complete New Guide to All the Birds of Eastern and Central North America.* 6th ed. Boston: Houghton Mifflin Harcourt, 2010.

Sibley, David Allen. *The Sibley Guide to Birds.* 1st ed. New York: Alfred A. Knopf, October 3, 2000.

"State of the Birds 2017: Key Findings." Mass Audubon, massaudubon.org/our-conservation-work/wildlife-research-conservation/statewide-bird-monitoring/state-of-the-birds/key-findings.

INDEX BY HOT SPOT

INDEX BY SPECIES

ABOUT THE AUTHOR AND PHOTOGRAPHER

Avid birders for many decades, best-selling author/photographer team **Randi and Nic Minetor** have produced more than forty books for FalconGuides and its parent company, Globe Pequot, including *Birding New England*, *Best Easy Bird Guide: Acadia National Park*, *The New England Bird Lover's Garden,* and *Backyard Birding: A Guide to Attracting and Identifying Birds.* Their work includes guides to a number of national parks and historic cities, as well as *Hiking Waterfalls in New York State*, *Hiking the Lower Hudson River Valley*, and *Hiking Through History New York.*

Nic's photography also appears in eight foldout Quick Reference Guides to the birds, trees, and wildflowers of New York City and New York State, and the trees and wildflowers of the Mid-Atlantic region. Randi is the author of six books that tell the true stories of people who have died in national and state parks: *Death on Mount Washington, Death on Katahdin, Death in Acadia National Park, Death in Glacier National Park, Death in Rocky Mountain National Park,* and *Death in Zion National Park.*

When not in the field, Nic is the resident lighting designer for Eastman Opera Theatre and the Memorial Art Gallery at the University of Rochester, and for theatrical productions at Rochester Institute of Technology and the National Technical Institute for the Deaf. Randi writes for a number of trade and medical magazines and serves as a ghostwriter for executives and entrepreneurs in a wide range of fields.